THROUGH THE YEARS

Published by:
Sun Point Press
P.O. Box 4711
Whitefish, MT 59937
sunpointpress.com

ISBN 978-0-982646304

Printed in the United States of America
First Edition/Fifth Reprint

Front Cover Photo
"Old Buses at Sherburne Lake"

Back Cover Photos
"Frank Liebig" (top right)
"Secretary Ickes"

The Glacier Association is pleased to make available the classic, **Through the Years in Glacier National Park**. **Through the Years** was originally published in 1960, reprinted in 1962, 1967, 1970, and 1973 but later went out of print. **Through the Years** is presented here unedited and unabridged, in its last printed version from 1973.

Bringing this classic back into print is just one of the many ways the Glacier Association fulfills its mission of **Advancing Stewardship of Our Natural and Cultural Heritage Through Education and Interpretation**. Funds generated by book sales in the visitor centers and proceeds from Glacier Association projects continue to provide important funding for interpretive materials and support for Glacier National Park.

The views expressed are reflective of the time and do not necessarily represent current perspectives of the National Park Service or the Glacier Association. Although times and culture change, this account of the park, has not. It is a timeless snapshot into the park we love.

Enjoy,

GLACIER ASSOCIATION
P.O. BOX 310
HISTORIC DEPOT
12544 HWY 2 E
WEST GLACIER, MT 59936
glacierassociation.org

THROUGH THE YEARS

in

Glacier National Park

★ ★ ★

An Administrative History

by

Donald H. Robinson
Formerly Assistant Chief Park Naturalist
at Glacier National Park

with Revisions by
Maynard C. Bowers
and
Richard W. Frost

★ ★ ★

Published by
Glacier Natural History Association, Inc.
In Cooperation with the
National Park Service

May, 1960

INTRODUCTION

"Land of Shining Mountains," the Indians called it. But there are many shining mountains in the United States, and the white men now have another name for this glorious land. They call it Glacier National Park.

This area in northwestern Montana lies astride the Continental Divide immediately adjacent to the Canadian boundary. Glacier National Park, encompassing an area of nearly 1600 square miles, was set aside as a representative sample of the most beautiful mountain scenery and of glaciation in the United States. It was set aside by an act of Congress in 1910 as a "pleasuring ground" for the American people and is the fourth largest of our twenty-nine national parks.

Hundreds of thousands of people visit the park each summer to enjoy the scenic splendor and relaxation afforded by this vast area of mountains, streams, and lakes. Yet we often wonder how many pause in their pleasurable pursuits to ponder upon the history of the area—for here the panorama of pageantry unfolds before us. A billion years or more ago the Belt seas deposited layer upon layer of sediments which were destined to become the buff, the green, the red, and other layers of the mountains. The Lewis overthrust built this range, only to have the glaciers scrape, pluck and grind away the rocks and carve out the valleys, cirques, aretes, and mountains.

Into this land then came the Indian; perhaps the legend of Napi will tell of the early beginnings. The story says that in the beginning Napi, Old Man of the Blackfeet, created the rocks and forests, the rivers, mountains, and prairie. He then made the animals and birds and fish. Then Napi molded a clay man and woman and gave them the breath of life. And he gave them dominion over all the creatures of the earth.

For a long time Napi dwelt among men, teaching them to fashion bows and arrows, tan hides, make shelters, use herbs, and know the magic of sacred objects. When man had learned how to take care of himself, Napi bade farewell to his beloved children. Then he returned to his home, the sun, going by way of Going-to-the-Sun Mountain. [1]

What did the area look like when white men first saw it, how was it established as a National Park, or how did the first park visitors reach the back country where one now drives a high-powered automobile over surfaced roads?

To fully answer these and other questions we must go back many years and delve into thousands of records, books, newspaper items, and other sources of information that have been deeply buried and long forgotten. Unfortunately much of the history of Glacier National Park has been lost because of lack of interest in its past and the scattering of written records.

Before we delve into the dim and faded records that lie before us, just a word of warning for those to whom the word "history" means merely a dull series of dates or a list of ancient peoples and places—this story is not meant for you. But if to you the history of an area is the re-creating of the past and the re-living of adventures and experiences long since gone—if the past is a living thing, a part and foundation of our present times, then you will surely enjoy the story of Glacier National Park's history that is to follow.

CHAPTER I

Discovery and Exploration

GEOGRAPHICAL SIGNIFICANCE

To appreciate fully the early political status of the area and the factors influencing early entry into it, one must know something of the peculiar geographical location of the park.

Sitting as it does astride the "Roof of the Continent," it is the one area in the United States that truly represents the dividing point between three major drainages—the Pacific Ocean, the Gulf of Mexico, and Hudson Bay. The early explorations into this part of the country also followed these same drainages, up the Mississippi-Missouri from American and French territories; up the Saskatchewan from British territory; and up the Columbia from British-American areas. As a result, the early ownership of the area now included in Glacier National Park was broken up into three divisions: that portion west of the Continental Divide, draining westward into the Columbia River; that east of the Divide, including the St. Mary, Belly River, and Waterton drainages, emptying into the Saskatchewan and Hudson Bay; and the remainder of the area, that laying south of St. Mary and east of the Divide, emptying into the the Missouri-Mississippi drainage.

TERRITORIAL CLAIMS AND OWNERSHIP

The history of territorial ownership in early North America was one of claims and counter-claims, treaties and disputes, until such time as the claimants of some particular area could get together and agree upon definite boundaries and ownership. Such was the early history of Glacier National Park. In one respect the story was more complicated than most other disputed territories in the United States because it centered around the three major continental drainages, all of which were in different hands and were reached by different routes of travel. In the days when travel and exploration naturally followed the major watercourses, this constituted three natural geographical regions, each with its own peculiar political problems.

Hudson's Bay Company

The first records we have of definite territorial claim to any part of what is now the park are found in the Hudson's Bay Company Charter. "The charter of Hudson's Bay Company gave it title to all the land drained by waters flowing into Hudson's Bay and Hudson Strait. Thus, at a pen stroke by the dissolute Charles II, in 1670 the story of the Hudson's Bay Company is first distantly linked to the history of Glacier, for the northern streams of the Park flow into Hudson's Bay and are hence within the area granted to the company." [2]

1

"This company was formed for the purpose of exporting to England furs and skins from British North America. The charter describes the company as 'the governor and adventurers of England trading into Hudson's Bay,' and consisted of Prince Rupert and seventeen noblemen. It invested complete lord-ship, including executive, legislative, and judicial powers, as well as exclusive trading rights. Its territory was defined as all lands watered by streams flowing into Hudson's Bay. Thus by royal decree the territory northeast of Triple Divide Peak became the southwestern corner of the grant." [3]

LaSalle

The next claim to any part of the park area was in 1682, when LaSalle made his famous exploration down the Mississippi River. "At this time he laid claim in the name of France, to all the waters drained by the Mississippi River, not realizing at the time the vast territory that he was claiming." [4]

This area comprises the part of the park lying east of the Continental Divide and south of Hudson Bay Divide.

Spanish Ownership

This portion of the park, claimed by LaSalle, remained in French hands until the Missouri-Mississippi territory was turned over to the Spanish, following the treaty of 1763 which ended the French and Indian War. This constitutes the second ownership of the southeastern corner of the park. However, this ownership did not remain long, for the land went back to France in 1800 at the secret treaty of San Ildefonso.

Louisiana Purchase

France did not retain her title to this territory very long, for on April 30, 1803, the Louisiana Purchase was consummated and the entire area west of the Mississippi and east of the Rocky Mountains, with the exception of the State of Texas and parts of Oklahoma, came into the possession of the United States. The area involved equaled approximately seven times the area of Great Britain and Ireland combined. The period of change, for this region, was by no means over because the ownership was still to change hands several times within the claims of new territories and states of the United States.

Louisiana Territory

The year following the Louisiana Purchase the area was divided into two parts, that lying south of the 33rd parallel being called the "Territory of Orleans," and that north of the parallel became little more than a geographical expression, known as the "District of Louisiana." This northern portion had no direct government, as such, until 1805 when it was raised to the rank of "territory," and was known as "Louisiana Territory," with its capitol at St. Louis.

Territory of Missouri

"In the year of 1812, the name 'Louisiana' passed to the state that now bears the name and the 'Territory of Louisiana' became the 'Territory of Missouri.'" [5] The new Missouri Territory included all the lands between the British possessions on the north and the 33rd parallel on the south, and from the Rocky Mountains on the west to the Mississippi River on the east. Thus the territory remained until pressure for state government, caused a break-up of the territory and the formation of the State of Missouri in 1821. The remainder of the territory north and west of the new state once again became unorganized Indian country and was without government until 1854.

Territory of Nebraska

By this time there was rapid settlement of the west and Congress was receiving increased pressure for the formation of new states and closer seats of government. Indians were becoming more and more careless about whose hair they helped themselves to, and troops and forts were requested. In 1854, this uncontrolled land was divided into two territories, Nebraska and Dakota, "the former embracing all lands north of the 40th parallel up to the 49th parallel and from the Missouri River to the Rocky Mountains, including what is now eastern Montana. This it remained until 1861." [6]

Dakota Territory

"On March 2, 1861, that part of the Nebraska Territory lying north of the 43rd parallel was made part of the Dakota Territory, thereby throwing the park area into still another political division. It was a vast territory, embracing all the area from the Red River to the Rockies, and from the Canadian Border to a line about the present boundary of South Dakota." [7]

Oregon Country

Now, for the sake of unity, let us leave the eastern slopes of the Rocky Mountains and find out what was happening across the mountains to the west. The treaty of 1818 between the United States and Canada established the International Boundary along the 49th parallel west to the summit of the Rocky Mountains. Until 1846, the so-called Oregon Country, embracing a vaguely defined area of the Pacific Northwest including what is now western Montana and the part of Glacier National Park west of the Continental Divide, was under the joint rule of the United States and Great Britain. In 1846, the division between United States and Canada was agreed upon at the 49th parallel, placing the Oregon Country under sole United States ownership. Then on August 14, 1848, Congress created the Oregon Territory, which included all of the area between the Rocky Mountains and the western sea, and between the 49th and 42nd parallels. Thus it remained until 1853 when this area was sub-divided, forming two territories, Oregon and Washington, the latter in-

3

cluding the present states of Washington, northern Idaho, and most of western Montana.

Idaho Territory

Due to still further demand for closer government, Congress passed a bill on March 3, 1863, creating the "Idaho Territory." Both Washington and Dakota gave land to form this new territory, which included all of what is now Idaho and Montana, and most of Wyoming. "The first name suggested for this new territory was 'Montana,' meaning 'land of mountains,' but this was objected to and the name 'Idaho' was substituted." [8]

Montana Territory

The new Idaho Territory was short-lived, though, because the finding of minerals caused a demand for still further government, and Congress was petitioned to form a new territory out of the eastern portion of Idaho. On May 26, 1864, Congress formed the Territory of Montana, much as it is found today, leaving the remainder to Idaho. There was an attempt to include only that portion of Montana lying east of the Rocky Mountains, but the people in the Bitterroot Valley objected and through the efforts of Sidney Edgerton, who later became the first governor of the Montana Territory, the western portion was also included.

State of Montana

"On November 8, 1889, President Harrison signed the bill admitting the 'State of Montana' to the Union." [9] This brought to a close an interesting crazy-quilt pattern of ownership of this small patch of rocks and scenery in the northern Rocky Mountains. Only one more major change now remained, that of the setting aside of Glacier National Park.

EARLY APPROACH TO THE AREA

Pre-History

"It is generally believed that the first human beings to reach North America came from Asia during the last great Ice Age, crossing the Bering Straits on the ice that covered it at that time. These people were probably nomadic tribes of Mongolian origin, looking for new lands over which to roam. It is also believed that these people first reached the plains country, where evidences are first found, by following down the eastern front of the Rocky Mountains, either over the ice or by way of an ice-free lane that existed at the same time that much of northern North America was covered by the last great ice sheet." [10]

By studying the ancient camp sites that have been found just south of the terminus of this last great glacier, archeologists can tell us much about the wanderings of these first citizens of this country. They also are able to

4

trace to some extent, the migration of these people from this area to other parts of the country. If this is true, and we have no reason to disbelieve it, we can assume that the area immediately east of Glacier National Park, and possibly even parts of the park, was visited by some of the first men to inhabit North America. It is doubtful that these early men went into the mountains, but they most certainly entered the foothills along the eastern front of the range as the vegetation and wild game followed the retreating ice sheet northward.

An old Piegan chief tells an interesting Indian legend depicting the origin of the Old North Trail, an ancient Indian trail extending along the entire eastern front of the Rocky Mountains from northern Canada to Mexico. "This old Indian, Brings-Down-The-Sun, stated that no one knew how long this trail had been used by the Indians, but that his father told him it had originated with the migration of a 'great tribe' of Indians from the distant north to the south, and all the tribes since that time had continued to use sections of it." [11]

When we stop to consider this legend, we realize how closely it ties in with the archeologists' findings, and it is not beyond the realm of possibility that this "great tribe" was the first migration of Mongolian peoples into the plains country of North America. If this is true, then Glacier National Park comes into still more prominence in the pre-history of the continent, for the remains of the Old North Trail can still be found in places, a very short distance east of the present park boundary, in the vicinity of East Glacier Park.

The present Blackfeet Indians that live on the reservation just east of the park, once controlled a vast area immediately east of the Rocky Mountains and were very jealous of any other tribe or white men entering this area. Unlike many of the other tribes of the west and the plains region, the Blackfeet have no clear-cut record of migration or origin. The only clue that we have to their probable origin is in their language, which is closely related to the Algonkian family language spoken only by the Indians of eastern North America. From this fact and certain legends, students of Indian culture have been led to believe that this once-great nation migrated from the east, probably through the Lake States, into southern Canada, and from there spread southward into Eastern Montana driving lesser tribes before them as they went.

"Culturally, the Blackfeet's closest kin are to the south, although he possesses many traits linking him with the Plateau area to the west and some linking him with the north. Linguistic and cultural comparisons, however, prove little as to origin of these people, for any or all of these may have come to them by diffusion and so imply nothing whatever as to tribal movements." [12]

Today the remnants of this great warrior nation reside on four reservations in southern Alberta and northern Montana, gradually losing the ways of their forefathers and taking on the dress, language, and ways of the white man.

5

The Coming of the White Man

The warlike Blackfeet Indians were a big factor in preventing the early trappers and traders from entering this area from the east. In addition, the great distances involved and the slow methods of transportation (mainly by canoe or other water craft) slowed the entry into eastern Montana and northern Wyoming. Yet, despite the hazards involved, the valuable furs to be found upon the upper reaches of the Missouri River brought adventuresome trappers and traders into the region early in the nineteenth century. They were quite successful in their efforts to push through the mountains south of the park, but attempts to penetrate into the country of the Blackfeet more often than not resulted in a "hair-raising" party, at which the Indians were more adept than the white man.

La Verendrye

It is believed that the first sighting of the Rocky Mountains was an outgrowth of an attempt by a party of French fur traders and adventurers under the leadership of Pierre Caultier de Varennes de la Verendrye, of Montreal, to reach the "western sea." La Verendrye spent several years, accompanied by his sons, pushing a line of trading posts westward from the Great Lakes, mainly in southern Saskatchewan plains. The elder Verendrye finally had to abandon his efforts and return to Montreal, but his two sons, Pierre and a younger brother, Francois de la Verendye, continued the effort. Finally, on their last trip westward, they made a great swing to the southwest and, on the first day of January, 1743, obtained their first sight of the eastern reaches of the Rocky Mountains, from a point believed to be in the southeastern part of the state of Montana.

It was long believed that they actually saw the main range of the Rocky Mountains from a point about the site of the City of Helena, but the discovery of a lead plate, in 1913, by some high school students on a bluff on the east bank of the Missouri River, opposite the City of Pierre, S. D., leads us to believe that they did not get as far as the "Gates of the Mountains." They perhaps saw the Big Horn Mountains and may have crossed the southeastern part of the state. This lead plate, inscribed with their names and the date, was recorded in their journal, along with a description of the mountains which they saw. The fact that the mountains were probably covered with snow at this time of year led Pierre and Francois to refer to them as the "Shining Mountains."

"Some historians believe that Pierre and Francois did not come closer than one hundred miles to these mountains, but other accounts record that, upon sighting the mountains, they turned west and traveled for twelve days, reaching the foot of the mountains, 'well wooded and very high.' This could also have been the Wind River Range, in Wyoming. In any event, we do know that this was the first recorded sight of the Rocky Mountains from the east." [13]

6

Peter Fidler

The next evidence of approach to the park area is found in the records of the Hudson's Bay Company, telling of a young surveyor, Peter Fidler, who was employed by them to map the area for their fur enterprises. In 1792 Peter Fidler left the Company's Buckingham House, in Canada, to winter with the Piegans, just east of the Rocky Mountains. While there he compiled considerable information about the mountains in the main range, which later appeared in the Arrowsmith maps of 1795. On these maps appeared "King Mountain," now known as Chief Mountain, and the Belly River. From these records we know that Fidler was acquainted with the eastern slopes of the park and we may conjecture that he may even have set foot within what we now call Glacier National Park. If so, he was the first white man to have done so.

Lewis and Clark

The next recorded approach to this area is found in the journals of Lewis and Clark, who passed to the south of the park on their way through the mountains to the mouth of the Columbia River. "On their westward journey, in 1805, Captain Meriwether Lewis ascended the Marias River some distance in order to determine which was the correct branch to follow, this or the Missouri proper. After ascertaining that this river followed too northerly a direction for their purposes, he returned to their camp at the forks of the rivers. Recognizing it as a major drainage in the area and a possible future route of trade, he named it the "Maria's River," in honor of his cousin, Miss Maria Wood." [14]

In July, 1806, upon their return from the coast, Captain Lewis and three men traveled upstream on the Marias River in an attempt to locate its source. On July 22, they reached a point where the course of the river turned southwestward, about twenty-five miles from the mountains. Here they remained for two days to make observations, but the weather was overcast and nasty, making astronomical observations impossible, and they were finally forced to the Missouri, after labeling this camp "Camp Disappointment." From here Lewis was able to look into what we know to be Marias Pass, and if he had continued undoubtedly he would have been the first white man to set foot in the pass. He makes no mention of the pass in his journals, though, which indicates that he did not realize what he had observed.

The location of Camp Disappointment is marked by a sandstone monument just off highway number 2, about two miles west of the station of Meriwether on the Great Northern Railroad near Cut Bank, Montana.

Marias Pass

Marias Pass, around the south end of the park, figures prominently in the early explorations of the area, along with Cut Bank (Pitamakan) Pass. It was due mainly to the search for easy passes through the mountains that much of

7

the later exploration was conducted. Marias Pass was one of the principal early passes through which the Indians from west of the mountains, mainly the Selish, (Flatheads) and Kootenais, came across the mountains to the buffalo hunting grounds in the country of the Blackfeet. Many early fur traders and prospectors also used this and other passes in the area, but, unfortunately, because too few left any record of their passing we know little of who they were, where they went, or when they passed. Indian warfare and ambushes eventually caused the western Indians to abandon general use of this pass forcing them to swing farther north to Cut Bank, Red Eagle, and other more difficult but safer routes of travel. Except for an occasional unrecorded crossing by trappers, miners, or others who left little record of their passing, Marias Pass did not again come into general use until its re-discovery in 1889 by John L. Stevens of the Great Northern Railway.

The first known use of Marias Pass by white men occurred in the year 1810 when David Thompson reported in his journals that a band of 150 Flathead Indians, accompanied by the white traders Finan McDonald, Michael Bourdeaux, and Baptiste Buch, crossed the mountains by a "wide defile of easy passage eastward of Selish (Flathead) Lake,"[15] to hunt buffalo and make dried provisions. As this was an early Indian pass and the most easily traversed, undoubtedly it was Marias Pass. Later accounts seem to bear this fact out, as does the decription of the trip and the following battle accounts. "At a spot believed to be just below the old railroad siding of Skyland, on Bear Creek, the party was attacked by 170 Piegans (Blackfeet) and a furious battle ensued. The Flatheads were forewarned, however, and had time to consolidate their positions, so that the Piegans were unable to inflict any damage and were finally driven off. Ambushes of this type were one of the reasons why this pass was not in general use at this time, and, although the Flatheads were quite jubilant over their decisive victory over the Piegans they did not again use this route for some time." [16]

The defeat of the Piegans by the Flatheads in Marias Pass angered the Blackfeet nation against the white man, possibly because there were white men along, but more probably because the western Indians were friendly to the white man and blamed him for furnishing the Flatheads and Kootenais with arms and ammunition to make war upon them. The Blackfeet served notice that any white men found east of the mountains would be considered as enemies and treated as such. The Flatheads did not help this situation any by boasting of their victory at Marias Pass.

In August of 1812, following an unsuccessful attempt at peace with the Piegans, the Flatheads went to their hunting grounds east of the mountains accompained this time by two free trappers, Michael Bourdeaux and Michael Kinville, both Frenchmen. On this trip they used the Cut Bank Pass, also one of their main routes of travel; but because the Piegans were guarding the

8

eastern approaches to the pass a terrific battle ensued. Many white men and Indians on both sides were killed and the Flatheads were forced to withdraw to do their hunting elsewhere. On Cut Bank Creek there is reported to be a great pile of stones covering the bones of a party of Flathead Indians who met defeat at the hands of the Piegans long ago, but no one knows where or when. Perhaps this is the site of the 1812 battle, and, if so, perhaps the bones of Bourdeaux, who fought so successfully against the Piegans in 1810, and of Kinville, rest there too.

Following the defeat of the Flatheads in Cut Bank Pass, the Piegans became even more warlike and set about relentlessly to wipe out any small bands of Indians that they could find. They set sentries at high points to watch over the eastern approaches to the passes, particularly Marias Pass, and every band that came through was ambushed and killed. Because of this, Marias Pass was, in effect, completely closed to all travel, necessitating still further use of the better protected passes farther north and south. This situation explains to some extent the failure of later expeditions to locate the pass, either because of the hostility of the Blackfeet nation or because of the natural reluctance of the western Indian guides to take parties through it. Thus, we find the one easy route to the Flathead Valley from the east effectively blocked to travel for the next seventy-five years, until even the trail was overgrown with grass and blocked by fallen timber. Only the more adventuresome attempted this route, and few left any record of their passing.

Hugh Monroe

Hugh Monroe was one of the earliest, if not the earliest, white man to see much of the area contained in the eastern portion of what is now Glacier National Park. There are many stories and legends concerning him and his doings, and many different dates are given for his birth and other events concerning his life in this part of the country.

Hugh Monroe was born in Quebec in 1798 (Canadian Archives), and came west at the age of sixteen to Fort Bow, on the Saskatchewan River, as an apprentice to the Hudson's Bay Company. When he arrived at the fort he expressed a keen interest in the Indians and a desire to learn their language. The Factor at Fort Bow, sensing his value to the company, and wishing to learn more of the inroads of the American fur companies to the south, sent Hugh to live for one year with the Piegans and learn their language. He was also told to scout for beaver trapping areas and to learn if there were any competing fur companies working in the Blackfeet country.

On the trip, which started in the fall of 1814, he was put under the care of Chief Lone Walker—who later was to become his father-in-law—of the Small Robes band of Piegans, and left with them for the south. Some historians state that it was while on this trip that Monroe first saw the St. Mary Lakes,

9

although others state that it was not until 1836 or even 1846. It is highly probable that, living as he did with the nomadic Piegans in the years to follow, he saw St. Mary Lakes long before 1836, and very likely in the years 1814 or 1815. If so, he was undoubtedly the first white man to set foot upon their shores.

Following his return from this first trip, he was sent again with them and this time apparently married his wife, Sinopah, daughter of Lone Walker. For the rest of his life he was to remain with the Blackfeet, a respected member of the tribe. Many descendants of Hugh still live on the plains of eastern Montana.

After Monroe went to live permanently with the Indians, he continued to serve the Hudson's Bay Company for some time, but later changed over to the employ of the American Fur Company. Still later, he left the American Fur Company to become a free trapper and trader, which status he held until his death. His friendly manner with the Indians made him an important factor in keeping peace between the white men and many bands of Piegans. He was also of considerable help to Governor Isaac I. Stevens of Washington Territory on the latter's survey trip of 1853, and is reported to have traveled extensively in the countries of the Flathead and Kootenai Indians.

Hugh Monroe died in December, 1892, and was buried at the Holy Family Mission of the Two Medicine River. Although his age, as reported on the burial records, was 109 years, a mathematical calculation from the records of the Canadian Archives indicated that he could not have been over 94 years old when he died.

The American Fur Companies

Following the entrance of the Hudson's Bay Company into the Blackfeet country, largely through the efforts of Hugh Monroe, there were many attempts by the American Fur Companies to establish trading posts at the headwaters of the Missouri River. A few free traders undoubtedly did meet with some success, but this area to the east of Glacier National Park was, for all practical purposes, a dead spot as far as the American companies were concerned. It was not until 1831 that Captain James Kipp was able to establish the first successful post on the mouth of the Marias River. This post, called Fort Piegan, was burned down the following year, but was rebuilt that fall and the name changed to Fort McKenzie. This post was soon followed by others, and marked the beginning of the end of the reign of the Blackfeet. Indian wars and strife followed, but the irresistible push of the fur traders, followed by the prospectors, could not be stopped.

Smallpox Epidemics

The dreaded disease, smallpox, was another decisive factor in breaking the strength of the Blackfeet Nation. "In the years of 1837 and 1838, this

10

disease ran rampant among the plains Indians of eastern Montana, and adjacent territories, brought into the country by one of the steamers on the Missouri, possibly the 'St. Peter' or the 'Assiniboine.' The epidemic appeared on the steamer on its way up river, and in passing one of the Mandan villages, an Indian is reported to have stolen a blanket from one of the sufferers. The disease immediately took hold in the village, and spread like wildfire, almost exterminating the tribe. From there it spread throughout the other tribes in the region, wiping them out like flies.

The accounts from the Blackfeet country, regarding the spread of this disease, were almost unbelievable. According to reports the number of Indians that died on the plains from this epidemic was between 60,000 and 150,000 victims. The wrath of the Indians toward the white man for bringing the disease into the country was understandable.'' [17]

Robert Greenhow

With the reports that began to filter back to the eastern states of these northern Rocky Mountains, with their furs and minerals, came a demand for more knowledge of the area. Fur companies and individuals wanted maps and reports of what conditions were like in this far-away land. As a result, maps were compiled from time to time, some from actual reconnaissance, some from the tales of early day adventurers, and some ''just compiled.'' One of the earliest maps and records of this area, after the Arrowsmith maps of 1795, was compiled by Robert Greenhow, an adventurous explorer who mapped the region in 1840 for the benefit of the fur companies. His map, published in 1850, as part of his ''Memoir Historical and Political of the Northwest Coast of North America,'' was remarkably complete and accurate, and showed the territories occupied by the various Indian tribes, the lakes, streams, and trading posts. On almost the exact location of the present Marias Pass he marked ''Route across the mountains.'' This is probably the earliest published record of this pass. Greenhow's information most likely came from accounts of the Indians that had used it, but nevertheless was astonishingly accurate.

Father DeSmet

At the same time that Greenhow was doing his exploration, another man who had a tremendous influence on the Indians of that day, although he never recorded setting foot in what is now Glacier National Park, started out from St. Louis for the west. The Jesuit priest, Father Pierre DeSmet, left St. Louis in April, 1840, to begin his missionary work among the Indians of the Northwest. He met an advance party of Flatheads on the Jefferson River and went with them into their country, the Bitterroot Valley. He spent many years with the Flatheads and other tribes of western Montana, Idaho, and Washington, and also worked some with the Blackfeet; his works were largely responsible for the acceptance of the white man by the western Montana tribes.

11

DeSmet knew Hugh Monroe and evidently traveled with him to some extent. James Willard Schultz states in his writings that Monroe took DeSmet to St. Mary Lakes and that the priest erected a cross there and gave them their name. However, various historians who have studied Father DeSmet's diaries and journals state that nowhere does he make mention of having entered what is now the park, nor does he make any mention of the St. Mary Lakes, which he most assuredly would have done had he seen and named them.

Our principal interest in DeSmet's work, though, concerns the influence that he had on the Indians, although when a question of war arose, many of the young bloods were often more than ready for the warpath, and the peaceful influence of the missionary was forgotten for the moment. Eventual settlement of the Indian's trouble was aided immeasurably by the early missionary teachings, but the history of white man-Indian relationships throughout the west is blackened by deeds on both sides that often tended to nullify the best efforts of those who worked so constantly for a peaceable solution.

EXPLORATION AND SURVEY

The period from 1850 to 1900 might well be called the period of discovery of Glacier National Park. Although, as has been previously shown, a few persons did set foot in the park prior to 1850, most of the effort of that time was spent in establishing a solid line of approach to these mountains. Now, for the first time, organized parties actually began to enter the mountains and to explore them. The railroad surveys, boundary survey parties, the United States Army, and various others interested in the region for one reason or another, pushed farther and farther into the area, finding new routes across the mountains and new wonders to record in their journals.

Boundary Surveys

One of the earliest penetrations of the park area was by the international boundary survey parties. With the settlement of the boundary disputes between the United States and Great Britain, plans were made to survey and mark the boundary dividing the two countries along the 49th parallel. In 1861 a survey party of the Northwest Boundary Commission, led by Archibald Campbell, and a corresponding British party, reached the Continental Divide and established a station on the northern end of the park, completing the first survey of the 49th parallel from the Pacific Ocean to the summit of the Rocky Mountains.

In March, 1872, President Grant signed the bill authorizing the remainder of the survey between the Lake of the Woods, Minnesota, and the summit of the Rocky Mountains, completing the boundary survey between the United States and Canada. In 1874, a survey party of the Northwest Boundary Commission completed the boundary survey from the east to the Continental Divide, connecting with the survey of 1861. The survey crew from Poplar River to the Divide was under the leadership of Captain Ames of the Sixth Infantry, who was accompanied by Dr. Elliott Cones and George Dawson, both of whom made botanical collections in the regions through which they passed. They camped on Waterton Lake for some time, and mapped the peaks and drainages in the area, but due to an error in the cartography of the Pacific Railroad Survey, they called the Waterton Lake, "Chief Mountain Lake," a name which correctly belonged to the Lower St. Mary Lake.

Baker Massacre

Just prior to the survey of the second section of the international boundary, there occurred a series of incidents that effectively put an end to the Indian troubles east of the mountains and paved the way for a steadily increasing number of exploration parties in the area. Malcolm Clark was one of the early Factors for the fur companies on the Missouri, who later located near Helena and kept a stage station on Prickly Pear Creek. In 1869, some Piegans arrived at the station and asked for Clark. When he appeared at the door, they shot him down and wounded his wife and one son. With the murder of Major Clark, friction arose between the whites and the Piegans, resulting in the so-called "Piegan War" which culminated in the Baker Massacre of 1870. There had been much friction and hard feeling, as well as bloodshed between the two factions for some time. Major Clark's murder, on the one hand, and the cold-blooded killing of Mountain Chief's brother and a young Blood Indian in the streets of Fort Benton, on the other hand, led to open warfare with the Piegans.

On January 19, 1870, following numerous Indian raids and agitation for action by Clark's two sons, Horace and Nathan, a column of cavalry and infantry under Brevet Colonel Eugene M. Baker, accompanied by the two Clark boys, left Fort Shaw to find Mountain Chief and his band of some fifteen hundred Blackfeet and settle this trouble once and for all. On the night of January 23, they came upon an Indian village in the dark and surrounded it, presumably thinking it was the camp of Mountain Chief, who was camped farther down the river. The camp was, in reality, a smallpox camp headed by Heavy Runner, an Indian who had been unswervedly friendly to the whites. Heavy Runner went out to meet the men and was shot down. The troops then descended upon the camp and massacred nearly everyone in it, which resulted, from official records, in 173 dead and 20 wounded, nearly all of whom were women an children or men too ill to defend themselves. Some reports state that Baker was informed when the shooting started that this was the wrong camp. Whether it be true or not, the fact remains that it was one of the blackest deeds perpetrated upon the Indians by the white men of this region.

The Baker Massacre, horrible though it was, marked the end of organized Indian uprising and opened the way for a period of safer access to the area now included in the park. This incident in a way, may be referred to as the instrument that opened the way for the mining and oil exploration period on the eastern slopes of the Rocky Mountains and that also gave free access to exploration of the area. Previous to this time, any explorers or other persons entering the Blackfeet Country were forced to keep their horses saddled and their powder dry. Any wandering bands of Blackfeet were eyed with suspicion and given a wide berth, if possible, for one did not know if they were friendly or not and chances were, they were not.

Woodruff and Van Orsdale

In the year 1873, Lt. Charles A. Woodruff and Lt. John T. Van Orsdale were ordered out from Fort Shaw with a small party of troops to make a reconnaissance to Fort Colville, in Washington Territory. On this trip, they followed Lewis and Clark's route on the way over, but on their return trip they decided to cross the mountains farther north. They followed up the Clark's Fork of the Columbia, passed near Flathead Lake, and thence up the Flathead River to the mouth of what is now Nyack Creek, presumably crossing by way of Cut Bank (Pitamakin) Pass.

The official files of the War Department record a report of Lt. Woodruff's of a trip by him and Lt. Van Orsdale into the Nyack Valley in 1863 and discovery of the glacier that was later located by Raphael Pumpelly and named for him (1873). Lt. Woodruff graduated from West Point in 1871, joined the 7th Cavalry, was wounded in the Battle of the Big Hole (1876) and promoted to Captain for his bravery there. He was also one of the first men to reach Custer's command after the massacre. [18]

John Kennedy

"In 1874 one John Kennedy, for whom Kennedy Creek is named, built a trading post at the junction of what is now Kennedy Creek and the St. Mary River, and did a good business for several years, after which he abandoned it and moved to the Sweetgrass Hills and later to Fort Benton and Great Falls." [19] This trading post is thought to be the first of its kind in the immediate vicinity of the park.

Duncan McDonald

In about the year 1878, Duncan McDonald, half-breed son of Angus Mc-Donald, visitel Lake McDonald, then known as Terry Lake. Duncan, who had the job of freighting a large amount of supplies to Canada, had intended to go up the North Fork of theFlathead, probably over the old Graves Creek Trail route but, upon finding the route blocked by a band of unfriendly Indians, he swung eastward, traveling the adjacent parallel valley, or Mc-Donald. At the close of the day, accompanied by his companions, a group of Selish Indians, he came upon this lake and camped there overnight. While in camp he carved his name upon the bark of a birch tree. The next day he continued his journey, reaching Canada safely.

The tree bearing his name remained for many years near the present village of Apgar. People who saw the name on the tree gradually began to call the lake "McDonald's Lake," and as such the name became fixed.

Just previous to this, in the same year, a famous Canadian Statesman, Sir John McDonald (no relation) is reported to have blazed a trail from the Canadian boundary to Terry Lake.

A few years prior to his discovery of Lake McDonald, Duncan was in charge of the Hudson's Bay Trading Post south of Flathead Lake. In 1874 he made his first trip through Marias Pass, in company with several Pend Oreille Indians. They traveled on snowshoes and chose this as the shortest route for McDonald from their camp on the Marias to his post on the Flathead. At the summit the Indians turned back, leaving McDonald and his Indian guide to continue alone. This trip showed that the pass could still be used and that it was still known and possibly used by the Indians at times. Later McDonald was to cross this pass several times, but, like so many before him, he left no record of his passing and several years were yet to come before the pass was located and put into general use by the Great Northern Railroad.

DUNCAN McDONALD

George Bird Grinnell

The year 1885 seems to have started a steady stream of explorers, hunters, miners, and the like into the mountains of Glacier. It was in that year that George Bird Grinnell, popularly known as the father of the movement to establish Glacier National Park, first came to the area. Inspired by articles written by James Willard Schultz for "Forest and Stream," a popular outdoor magazine of which he was editor, Grinnell made his first trip to the area. From Helena where he arrived via the Northern Pacific Railroad, he took the stage to Fort Benton, and a wagon from there to the Blackfeet Agency at Badger Creek. From there he and Schultz traveled by saddle horse and duffel wagon to the St. Mary Lakes, presumably along the Old North Trail. Here the men hunted and explored for some time, but did not get any farther than the

15

Upper St. Mary Lake. Grinnell left that fall with the vow to come again and see more of the region.

Grinnell returned to the area in 1887, this time traveling up the Swiftcurrent valley to what is now known as Swiftcurrent Lake. While encamped in this valley, he discovered the glaciers at the heads of Swiftcurrent and Grinnell Valleys. Accompanied by Lt. Beacon and James Willard Schultz, he climbed to the glacier that now bears his name to explore and photograph it. There is some difference of opinion regarding the person that named the glacier after Grinnell, both Schultz and Beacon claiming the honors, but Beacon's diary and correspondence between himself and Grinnell seem to throw the honors toward Beacon.

Grinnell returned annually to the area for many years and recorded the abundance of game animals that were to be found there. Many of the names of features on the eastern slopes of the park were given as the result of some incident or person involved in the big game hunts in the vicinity.

Being interested in the natives of the western plains, Grinnell studied the Blackfeet Indians and became an authority on them. He was adopted as a member of the tribe, and was given the name of Pinut-u-ye-is-tism-o-kan (the Fisher Cap). At the petition of these people, he was appointed to negotiate with them concerning the governmental acquisition of the area east of the Continental Divide. This region was purchased in 1891 and was thrown open to prospectors. However, as soon as the mining excitement subsided, Grinnell pointed out the prudence of setting aside this mountainous country as a national preserve. An article by him, "The Crown of the Continent" published in "Century Magazine" in 1901 became a milestone on the way to the establishment of the park. After nineteen years of endeavor, the act establishing Glacier National Park was passed by Congress in 1910, and the park became a reality. It will always be regarded as symbolic of the resourcefulness, foresight and untiring effort of this man. To George Bird Grinnell the people of Montana and the entire nation owe a debt of gratitude.

Lt. Robertson

"In the summer of 1886, Lt. S. R. Robertson made a reconnaissance trip from Fort Assiniboine, on the Milk River, to the St. Mary area, traveling as far as the head of Lower St. Mary Lake." [20] On this trip he mapped the area along the eastern face of the mountains, showing many of the peaks and rivers with the names that they carry to this day.

Lt. Ahern

In August of 1890, Lt. George P. Ahern, then stationed at Fort Shaw on the Sun River, was ordered to take a detachment of soldiers and explore the

17

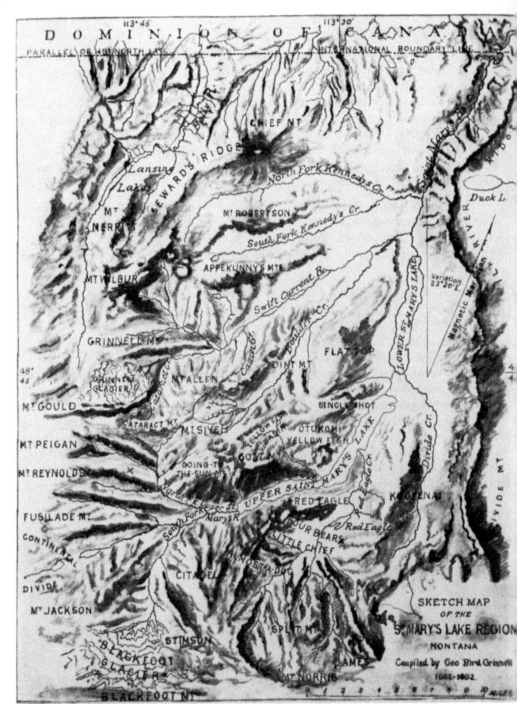

GEORGE BIRD GRINNELL'S MAP

18

mountains north of Marias Pass. The party consisted of Ahern, a detachment of Negro soldiers from the 25th Infantry, Professor G. E. Culver of the University of Wisconsin, two mountaineers, packer and guide respectively, two prospectors, and two Indian guides and the pack train. The party left Fort Shaw on August 5, crossed the prairies, and finally reached the foot of the mountains near Cut Bank Creek. From there they went north to the International Boundary, thence up the Belly River to the pass that was later named for Lt. Ahern.

Upon reaching this pass the entire party worked for two days making a trail from the foot of the talus slope to the summit, completing the first of two known successful trips with pack stock over Ahern Pass. (The second trip was by R. H. Sargent of the U. S. Geological Survey, in 1913). Because the western slope of the pass was heavily timbered they had difficulty cutting their way through. They were not helped by the fact that most of the trip was accomplished in pouring rain.

Upon reaching McDonald Creek they turned up the creek for some distance, then crossed over into the Camas Creek Valley, probably in the vicinity of the present Heaven's Peak Lookout Trail. From there they traveled down Camas Creek (which he calls Mud Creek on his map) to the valley of the North Fork of the Flathead River, where they swung back toward Lake McDonald, presumably about the route of the present North Fork Truck Trail, and proceeded down the Flathead River to the Flathead Valley.

Side trips were made on this journey up the Cut Bank Creek to the summit, up the Swiftcurrent Valley or St. Mary Valley—the records are not clear on this—to the summit, and over the Continental Divide from McDonald Creek into the headwaters of the Waterton Valley. The complaints of present day "dude" parties about trail conditions seem silly in the face of the difficulties faced by these men who had to cut a route through a virgin forest and in many instances to build a trail in order to get their stock through. To appreciate this fully, one would have to attempt taking loaded pack stock cross-country from Ahern Pass to Camas Creek today—a feat that modern packers would term practically impossible.

Henry L. Stimson

As a young man Henry L. Stimson, who was later to become the Secretary of War, and one of the nation's important personages, made several trips into what is now Glacier National Park on hunting and exploration expeditions. In 1891 he was a member of the party that discovered the mountain that was later to bear his name. Also, in 1892 he and Dr. Walter B. James of New York, accompanied by an Indian guide named "Indian Billy," ascended the east face of Chief Mountain. Upon reaching the summit they found the remains of an old bison skull, practically all decayed except for the frontal bone and

19

the horn stubs, securely anchored on the highest point and protected from the wind by rocks.

The Piegan Indians tell of one of their young men who, while on a hunting party bragged that he could climb this peak. He started up from the west side, and when last seen by his friends was still climbing. He was never seen again, and the Blackfeet thereafter avoided very close contact with the mountain.

CHIEF MOUNTAIN

The Flathead Indians tell of one of their braves who, when it came time to take his warrior's sleep and make himself ready for his "medicine vision," went across the mountains taking a sacred bison skull for a pillow. There he climbed to the top of the large mountain overlooking the plains and stayed for days, fasting and praying until he had received his vision that was to govern his later life. Then he returned, leaving the skull on the mountain top. Could not this be the true explanation of the skull found by Stimson on Chief Mountain? For how else could the skull have been carried there when no white man had previously set foot on this peak and most certainly no bull bison had climbed it? And we must marvel at the spirit and courage that motivated this brave to ascend this peak and stay there when we know of the

20

awe with which these primitive people regarded these high, silent, and even more savage peaks.

Early Settlement of Western Slopes

We now drop back a few years to start at the beginning of the white man's entry into the western side of the park. Even though the Indians were more friendly on the west, there seemed to be little incentive for the white man to enter the western valleys that led toward the summit of the Rocky Mountains. Occasionally a party passed through the area on its way across the mountains, but few made any extensive stay in the area.

Lt. A. W. Tinkham led an exploration party for Governor Stevens up the Nyack Valley and over the Cut Bank Pass in 1853, and others crossed various passes from time to time, leaving little or no record. Lts. Ahern and Woodruff took parties through the area and Duncan McDonald most certainly spent some time in the Lake McDonald area on his expeditions through the mountain passes. But it was not until the coming of the Great Northern Railroad in 1892 that people began to enter the region around Lake McDonald and settle there. From that time on, settlement of the region was rapid and exploration and development of the park area were carried on with enthusiasm.

ORIGINAL APGAR CABIN

21

DR. LYMAN B. SPERRY

Among the first to arrive in the Lake McDonald area was Milo B. Apgar, who reportedly came over Marias Pass with his belongings in a two-wheeled cart and settled at the foot of Lake McDonald on the spot that was later to bear his name, the present village of Apgar. With him came Charles Howe, for whom Howe Ridge is named. These two men homesteaded at the foot of the lake and very shortly were in the "dude" business. Apgar immediately began to build cabins on the site of the present Village Inn at the little village of Apgar and furnished overnight accommodations for the visitors who were to come through on their way up Lake McDonald and into the park.

Charles Howe is reported to have been the first person to sight Avalanche Lake and Sperry Glacier from near the summit of Mt. Brown in August of 1894. Upon spotting the lake, he retraced his steps and reached the lake by skirting the western and northern slopes of the mountain. Howe was so enthusiastic about his find that he reported it to Dr. Sperry on his trip into the area the next year. It was from his description that Dr. Lyman B. Sperry, the "Gentleman Explorer," came to explore the Avalanche Lake Basin and actually to reach and set foot upon Sperry Glacier.

Dr. Lyman B. Sperry

Dr. Sperry, a professor from the University of Minnesota, arrived in the park in 1895, about the time that Howe had discovered the best route to Avalanche Lake. Upon hearing about the lake and glacier, he became interested and organized a party to explore the area. "On the third of June, 1895, a party consisting of Professor J. Paul Goode, Messrs E. R. Shepard (photographer), W. O. Jones, and W. A. Wittick, of Minnesota, and the writer (Dr. Sperry)—all under the guidance of Frank Geduhn, one of the early settlers at Lake McDonald—penetrated the thick and tangled forests between Brown's Peak and Goat Mountain (Mt. Brown and the present Mt. Cannon), entered the deep valley and camped on the lake shore. Our party carefully noted the most striking features of the locality, photographed its more conspicuous points, and because of the number of avalanches seen and heard during our stay, agreed that Avalanche Basin would be a most appropriate name for the place.

"Finding that a single day in this remarkable place could give but a taste of its delights, some of our party determined to visit again as soon as practicable. During the latter part of July a passable saddle and pack trail was cut from the head of Lake McDonald to the foot of Avalanche Lake, and on the first day of August, accompanied by Professor L. W. Chaney of Carleton College, and Mr. A. L. Sperry of Owatonna, Minnesota, I, (Dr. Sperry) made a second visit to the region."

"We had expected to be the first to pass over the trail on horseback into this wild retreat, but Mr. J. H. Edward, of Kalispell, with his wife and

23

SPERRY PARTY AT AVALANCHE LAKE

brother, reached the lake a few hours ahead of us, having followed immediately upon the heels of the trail-makers. Mrs. Edwards, therefore, enjoys the distinction of being the first woman to visit Avalanche Basin." [21]

According to Alfred L. Sperry, in his book, "Avalanche," the party did continue on up the McDonald Valley and eventually reached the area now known as Granite Park and Ahern Pass. While there they climbed the Garden Wall and looked down upon Grinnell Glacier, and also walked out upon a glacier near Ahern Pass which they named for Dr. Chaney.

It was not until the year 1896 that Dr. Sperry was able actually to set foot upon his glacier, reaching it the first time by the Avalanche Lake route, but later by way of Snyder and Sprague Creeks, much as it is reached today.

It was at this time that the good Doctor also saw the possibilities of a trail to the glacier and mountainous region east of Lake McDonald. With this in mind, he conferred with James J. Hill, president of the Great Northern

24

Railroad, to work out a plan whereby he could bring college students into the area to build this trail.

SPERRY PARTY ON SPERRY GLACIER

By 1902 he had reached an agreement with the railroad whereby the Great Northern would furnish transportation to and from the park, tents, food and supplies, and Dr. Sperry would recruit students from the University of Minnesota to do the work, without wages, for the opportunity of spending a summer in the mountains. The summer of 1902 saw some 15 students hard at work on the project, and by the end of 1903 the trail was completed to the east side of Gunsight Pass, with a side trail to the headwall below Sperry Glacier. Dr. Sperry laid out the trail and supervised the job in general, but E. E. (Billy) Ellsworth acted as trail foreman, with J. E. (Eddie) Cruger and his stepfather, Danny Comeau, packing supplies to them from Lake Mc-Donald. Although this trail was rebuilt in later years by the National Park Service, it is a monument to Dr. Sperry's engineering ability that even today varies little from the original trail.

With the coming of the railroad the days of true exploration were practically over, and few major areas remained where someone had not already set foot. The railroad and later the automobile roads brought explorers of another sort, those seeking benefits and experiences other than those achieved solely by being first in an area. To these people we are indebted for the support which they gave and which is still needed to maintain these primitive areas in their natural condition.

THE COMING OF THE RAILROADS

With the settlement of the western coast of North America and the organization of local and territorial governments in the area, came an almost frantic rush by railroad companies to push their rails to the western sea and tap the growing amount of trade in the newly opened regions. The Union Pacific and others following the more southerly routes were soon traveling to the west coast but for one reason or another the territories farther north were unable to obtain this mode of transportation for some time.

Much of the early history of Glacier National Park centers around the search for easy railroad passes through these northern mountains and particularly for the elusive "route through the mountains" which we know now as Marias Pass. For over thirty-five years various persons in an official capacity searched for this pass, while at the same time other people—trappers, traders, and prospectors—were aware of the pass and often using it without the knowledge of the former.

Stevens Expedition — 1853-54

When the Washington Territory was formed in 1853 and Isaac I. Stevens was appointed governor of this new territory, the first job assigned to him was to make a survey of possible railroad routes into the northwest, along the northern border of the country. He immediately formed his party for the survey and set out for the west, arriving at Fort Benton, on the upper reaches of the Missouri in the late summer of 1853.

Because of the lack of guides at Fort Benton who were acquainted with the mountains to the north, and also because of their reluctance to venture into the Blackfeet Country with such a party, Stevens' men were forced to use Indian guides or the few white men who knew the plains country east of the mountains. Among those hired for this work was Hugh Monroe, who acted both as guide and interpreter for A. W. Tinkham, one of the party's chiefs of survey. Tinkham's party scouted north from Fort Benton toward the Canadian line but was not successful in locating any pass through the mountains. Why his guides did not lead him to Marias Pass will probably never be known, for surely Monroe at least knew of its existence. But here again the warlike attitude of the Blackfeet entered into the picture. It is reported that throughout the entire trip Monroe seemed uneasy and was constantly on the lookout for war parties. Despite the fact that he lived with them and married into the tribe, he seemed to be aware of the danger surrounding a lone party of white men invading Blackfeet territory. Possibly that is one of the reasons why the party did not locate the pass from the east.

While at Fort Benton, Governor Stevens was told of the existence of an easy pass between the Blackfeet country and the land of the Flatheads by one of the friendly Blackfeet chieftains, Little Dog. This fired Stevens to continue the search for the pass but, as winter was fast approaching, he was forced to continue to his winter camp that was being established by Lt. Saxton in the Bitterroot Valley.

Upon reaching his winter camp in the early fall of 1853, Stevens found that the winters were not so severe as he had been led to believe, so he decided to send Tinkham up from the west side of the mountains to look again for this lost pass. Tinkham requested Monroe and another white guide, Dauphin, to accompany him, but they refused. Perhaps it was because of the rumors of several bands of Blackfeet raiding on both sides of the mountains that they would not venture into the area, but returned to Fort Benton by a southern route.

Tinkham was not to be deterred by the refusal of the guides nor by the reports of war parties; he secured the services of a lone Flathead guide and set out, traveling up the Flathead Lake and the Middle Fork of the Flathead River to what is now known as Nyack Creek. Here the guide, for reasons known only to himself, turned off up Nyack Creek and led the party over Cut Bank (Pitamakin) Pass. Possibly, at this time, the lower route over the Marias was impassable for horses because of lack of use, or maybe he was a little afraid of the Blackfeet raiding parties east of the pass. At any rate it was not until October 19 in bitter cold and flying snow that they reached the vicinity of Cut Bank Pass, having covered over two hundred miles in twelve days, the last eight miles of which took seven days. On the following day, they crossed the pass and proceeded down toward Fort Benton. From there Tinkham traveled back to the winter camp and reported to Stevens that the pass was impractical for locating a railroad. His is the first accurately recorded journal of a trip through what is now the park.

When Governor Stevens returned from his expedition in the spring of 1854, he evidently felt that Tinkham's findings were not complete or that the pass mentioned by Little Dog was still undiscovered, so he left another of his lieutenants, James R. Doty, at Fort Benton to continue the search. Doty and his party immediately set out for the eastern front of the range, from there then turned north along the immediate foothills toward the Canadian boundary, following the Old North Trail as far as Bow (St. Mary) and Chief Mountain (Lower St. Mary) Lakes. Upon his return he turned west and followed the upper Marias River (Now the South Fork of the Two Medicine) almost to its source. There he is reported to have climbed a hill where he could look into a low pass through the mountains (Marias). As he was under orders to be back to Fort Benton by June, he did not go any farther. Upon his return to Fort Benton, maps were made of the trip showing the pass, and plans were laid to return and continue the survey. Unfortunately, however, these plans were cancelled by Jefferson Davis, then Secretary of War, who felt that enough money had been wasted in this very long-drawn-out search for a mythical pass through the mountains. Doty was very disappointed at this turn of events. Had he been allowed to continue the survey, the history of the area might again have taken a vastly different turn. By such minor events is the history of our country often governed.

Blackfeet Treaty

In October 1855, after many conferences with different Indian tribes of the northwest, Governor Isaac Stevens held a great council at the mouth of the Judith River and established the Blackfeet Reservation. This treaty included many tribes both east and west of the Rocky Mountains. The purpose of this and the other treaties signed with the other tribes was to promote peace and establish common hunting grounds among the tribes. The Blackfeet Treaty, which established a hunting ground on the Blackfeet Territory for eastern Indians but prevented the Indians west of the mountains from using the passes in or near what is now the park, really touched off the fireworks. The treaty was immediately condemned by the western Indians and was never kept by them. The result was a period of almost continual strife and warfare between the tribes between 1855 and 1870.

The prime significance of this treaty is the fact that it stopped, for the next fifteen years, further attempts to enter the part of the Rocky Mountains now occupied by the park until after the quieting of Indian troubles following the Baker Massacre.

Palliser Expedition

About this same time the British Government north of the Canadian Boundary was also becoming interested in the possibility of rail routes across the mountains. In the year 1857 they sent John W. Palliser with an expedition to explore the western part of Canada and to look for possible railroad passes through the mountains. The southern division of this party under the command of Lt. T. W. Blakiston was directed to operate along the boundary. In the year 1858 it entered the area now encompassed by Waterton Lakes National Park, immediately north of Glacier National Park. There they camped on Waterton Lakes and so named them for Charles Waterton, an eminent naturalist. Members of this party may have been the first white people to see these lakes or at least to leave any record of having been there.

From the Waterton Valley the party crossed the Continental Divide by one of the passes north of the boundary, possibly South Kootenai Pass, and continued westward to the Tobacco Plains Country, near the present site of Eureka, Montana. This trail, used extensively in later years by both Indians and white men, extended from the Old North Trail near the foot of Waterton Lake over the South Kootenai Pass, across the northwestern corner of the park, thence over the Whitefish Divide by way of Yak-in-i-kak and Graves Creeks, to the Tobacco Plains country. From there trails continued to Fort Colville and Walla Walla in the Washington Territory. In the early days this was one of the main routes between the eastern Washington region and the plains of southern Alberta.

The survey maps of both Doty and Blakiston were very complete and surprisingly accurate when compared with modern maps. Much of Doty's route can be retraced from his narrative description of the geographic features he encountered. Blakiston's map showed for the first time many of the old Indian trails across the mountains, as well as the streams, peaks and rivers in considerable detail. These maps and reports were to furnish the basis for further and more detailed exploration in the following years.

Old North Trail

An interesting sidelight to the study of this area is the existence of the different trails that reached from one place to another. Without the aid of the well-traveled Indian trails much of the exploration of this area would have been impossible or at least much more difficult. From time to time mention is made of trails through the mountains. The longest and most heavily used of them all was the "Old North Trail." This was one of the longest, if not the longest, continuous trail in the west. Blackfeet Indian legends tell of a group of Blackfeet that once decided to visit the people in the south and started out along the trail, traveling for twelve months, until they reached the country of the "people with dark skins and hair falling over their face" (Mexico). They were gone, in all, four years on this trip.

This Old North Trail, into which all of the east-west trails led, evidently extended from Mexico, or near there, north to the vicinity of the present city of Calgary, along the eastern face of the Rocky Mountains. At Calgary it branched, one trail continuing along the mountains and the other leading northeast into the Barren Lands as far as people lived. Evidences of this trail could be found until recent years, and probably might still be located if searched for diligently. And it was this network of trails throughout the nation that led the early explorers into these areas, crossing and re-crossing, much as our highways and railroads do now.

Hamilton and McKay

In 1858, Governor Stevens was concerned about the Indian trouble that resulted from the Judith Basin Treaty of 1855. Because no further reconnaissance could be made into the area until this was quelled, he sent two men, William T. Hamilton and Alex McKay, disguised as trappers and traders, into the Blackfeet country to learn the attitude of the Blackfeet toward the trouble. The two men managed to reach the camp of Little Dog, who was still friendly toward the white men, although his people were not. From there they went on and, upon reaching the second camp of Indians, found a very unfriendly welcome awaiting them. In attempting to leave this camp, a fuss was stirred up, a few of the Indians were killed, and Hamilton and McKay left as fast as they could go.

When they reached the vicinity of St. Mary Lake, they fell in with a band of Kootenai Indians from west of the mountains. As soon as the whites arrived, the Kootenais, knowing full well what was to happen, broke camp and retreated as rapidly as possible toward Red Eagle Pass and the safety of the western slopes of the mountains but were overtaken by the Blackfeet just below the main pass where a furious battle resulted. The Blackfeet were repulsed with heavy losses. Undoubtedly Hamilton and McKay had plenty to report to Stevens upon their return.

Fort Benton and Kootenai Wagon Road

Despite later search for the pass, the existence of Marias Pass was known by this time from the reports of traders and others, as well as from the maps and reports of Doty. As further concrete evidence of this, "the first legislative assembly of the newly created territory of Montana convened at Bannock, the territorial capital on December 12, 1864. Here they passed an act to incorporate the 'Fort Benton and Kootenai Road Company,' empowering the company to build a wagon road from Fort Benton through Marias Pass, to intersect with the 'Hell Gate and Kootenai Wagon Road, about thirty miles above the head of Flathead Lake (probably in the vicinity of Columbia Falls or Whitefish). The road was to be paid for by a levy of toll charges for the different amounts and types of traffic that used the road. The act was signed by the first territorial governor, Sydney Edgerton, on February 2, 1865, but Indian trouble, including a massacre on the Marias River, broke up the plans for the road and it was abandoned before it was started.

Provisions of the act empowered the company to erect a toll gate at Marias Pass and collect tolls as follows: For each wagon, four horses or more, $8.00; for each wagon drawn by less than four animals, $5.00; for pack animals and horsemen, $1.00 each; for loose animals, mules, etc., fifty cents. The act further provided that the road be built within two years, and after completion, be kept in good repair for travel." [22]

30

Northern Transcontinental Railway Survey

"In the year 1881 one Henry Villard, backed by the Northern Pacific Railroad and the Oregon Railway and Navigation Company organized what he called the Northern Transcontinental Railway Survey, to make a complete survey of the northwestern country, with the view of development by these railroads and others. To head this survey, he called upon the eminent geologist Raphael Pumpelly. As a crew to carry out this survey, he selected the following men, most of whom were then or later, big names in their respective fields:

A. D. Wilson, topographer   F. A. Gooch, chemist
Bailey Willis, geologist   Prof. Charles Sargent, forester
Boyard Putnam, geologist   Prof. E. W. Hilgard, soils
J. E. Wolff, geologist   W. B. Canby, plants and range con-
George Eldridge, geologist   ditions
Waldeman Lindgren, geologist

W. R. Logan was hired as head packer. This survey carried on through 1882 and 1883, resulting in Mr. Pumpelly's crossing of Cut Bank Pass in 1883." [23]

In the spring of 1882, Professor Pumpelly and his crew headed west and started their survey. In the early summer the professor and his party, including W. A. Stiles, a newspaper man, and Major Logan, who later was to become the first Superintendent of Glacier National Park, attempted to cross Cut Bank (Pitamakin) pass from the east, but upon reaching the pass were turned back by the tremendous snow banks still remaining from the previous winter's snowfall. Upon their return they continued their survey and reached the western side of the Rocky Mountains in 1883. Again the party attempted the pass, this time in August, from the western side, and were successful.

On this latter attempt they traveled cross-country from the Bitterroot Valley, up the Flathead River to Lake McDonald, where they struck an old Indian trail leading over the pass. On this trip they located what was later named Pumpelly Glacier from a place called Mud (Nyack) Creek. It was also on this trip that they climbed Mt. Stimson. "Professor Canby's diary records visits to 'Van Orsdale's Flume and 'Woodruff's Falls' on Nyack Creek, near Mt. Stimson, while Pumpelly and others were climbing to the glacier. This record verifies Woodruff's and Van Orsdale's prior discovery (1873) of the glacier. This pass was called 'Marias' Pass in newspaper accounts of the day." [24]

Great Northern Railway

Up to this time the interest of the railroads in the area was confined to searching for passes and surveying possible routes. Roads farther south were rapidly pushing their rails westward, but so far there had been no sign of rails reaching the area of Glacier National Park. In the year 1878 James J. Hill and several associates bought out a bankrupt "streak of rust" in Minnesota, a land grant railroad known as "St. Paul and Pacific." The new management, which included George Stephens, president of the Bank of Montreal, and Donald A. Smith, chief commissioner of the Hudson's Bay Company, reorganized and renamed it the "St. Paul, Minneapolis, and Manitoba Railway Co.," later renamed the "Great Northern Railway Co." By 1883 Hill, as general manager, had started pushing the rails of this budding giant westward toward the Pacific Ocean. In the year 1887 the road reached Great Falls and Helena. Hill had hoped for a pass through the Rockies in the region near the Canadian border, but his locating engineers had failed to find the elusive passage known as Marias Pass. The lack of accurate maps of the pass probably prevented him from building directly toward it in the first place, from Pacific Junction (just west of Havre). Hill employed a young engineer, John F. Stevens (no relation to Governor Isaac Stevens) to locate this elusive pass and decide upon the feasibility of constructing the line through it, thereby reducing the rail distance between St. Paul and the coast, and at a much lower grade than in the Butte region of the Rocky Mountains.

To John F. Stevens is often given the credit for "discovering" Marias Pass. Perhaps we should better say, he explored it for the Great Northern Railway. Since Finan McDonald crossed it in 1810, there were numerous white men and hundreds of Indians known to have crossed it at one time or another. Knowing this but not having an accurate map of it, is probably what led James J. Hill to send Stevens in search of the pass, with the establishment of the railroad in mind. From various reports it seems evident that Hill's orders to Stevens were based upon reports by Major Marcus D. Baldwin. Baldwin stated that when he first arrived in the Flathead he had entered Marias Pass from the west, explored it thoroughly, and then he reported his findings to Mr. Hill. His report, perhaps coupled with the old maps of Doty and Robertson, undoubtedly were the deciding factors in sending Stevens to locate the pass and determine its feasibility as a railroad pass. In any event, in December of 1889 Stevens accompanied by a Flathead Indian by the name of Coonsah, started out to locate the pass. It was bitterly cold and Coonsah finally played out and had to be left behind. Stevens proceeded alone in a blizzard and by evening had reached the pass and crossed it far enough to be certain that it was the true pass and that it was useable. It being too late to return that night to the camp where he had left Coonsah, he remained in the pass until morning, tramping back and forth in a runway beaten out of the snow to keep from freezing. The next morning, upon returning to the camp where he had left the Indian, he found that Coonsah had allowed the fire to go out and was almost frozen to death. After Stevens revived the Indian they returned to the Blackfeet Agency on Badger Creek from which they had started. A statue at Summit in Marias Pass commemorates Stevens' exploration of this pass.

STATUE OF STEVENS AT MARIAS PASS

The following spring, survey crews headed for the pass and the last lap in the construction of the Great Northern Railway to the coast was under way. A tote road was built through the mountains and construction camps were set up. The tote road itself was a major undertaking, and following the path of least resistance and steepness of grade was no obstacle. Many of the trees along the old road for many years showed the marks where ropes were snubbed around them to lower heavily loaded wagons down the grades. The Flathead River had to be forded in two places; this was a hazardous venture during high water.

Following the survey and grading crews, which were now well on their way to the coast, the track-laying crews on the Great Northern started out from the town of Cut Bank on April 24, 1891. The summit of the Rocky Mountains at Marias Pass was reached on September 14 and Kalispell on the last day of the year, 1891. By April, 1892, the road had reached the western border of the state, and in 1893 the first transcontinental trains started rumbling across the pass.

The building of this road was accompanied by the inevitable line of wild construction towns, the wildest of which was McCarthyville, located about five miles west of Summit, and at one time considered the toughest town in the state of Montana. "Slippery Bill" Morrison, a noted character of those times, earned his nickname from the fact that he was able to spend one entire winter in McCarthyville and come out in the spring with a whole skin, despite his good luck at poker playing. "Slippery" is reported to have stated that when the snow went off that spring nine bodies were discovered, as mute evidence of the moral code of the town.

OLD McCARTHYVILLE

With the completion of the railroad through Marias Pass, development of the area was rapid. Shortly after reports reached the outside regarding the beauty of the area, the first "dudes" began to arrive in ever-increasing numbers and started this mountain region along its path of catering to summer visitors, a business that is still increasing.

Railroad Surveys on the North Fork of the Flathead

The story of the railroads would not be complete without a mention of the railroad surveys that were made on the North Fork of the Flathead River in 1909. The park was about to be created, and there was a possibility of finding in the area, coal and oil in sufficient quantities to make the need for a road imperative. What probably precipitated the surveys was the appearance of a rival railway company upon the scene. At any rate, in the year 1909, the Great Northern Railway and the Milwaukee Railroad ran surveys for the right-of-way of the North Fork of the Flathead to the Canadian line. Each company rushed to complete the survey first, file its plats of the survey, and thereby get the franchise for a road.

These surveys were a hard-fought battle between the two rival crews. When one crew got behind, they would drop over onto the survey of the other and use it until they caught up and then take to the woods again. If a road had been built up there, one wonders how much good these surveys would have been.

As the work extended through most of the following winter, the crews had to be supplied by pack trains, both up the west side of the river and through the park. Some of the packers had to use snowshoes on their horses and others travois, in order to get the supplies through. Undoubtedly the men had hard going at times and occasionally they were a little hungry, but they carried on until recalled by their respective companies.

And so another era in the development of the park comes to a close. The appearance of the steam engines with their long strings of passenger and freight cars take the mountains a long way from the unexplored wilderness that it had been such a short time before. And the hordes of visitors that poured into the mountains in the years to come, now that modern transportation was available, marked the beginning of a demand for preservation of the area and the creation of a National Park.

THE MINING AND OIL PERIOD

Early Mining Ventures

The quieting of the Indian troubles in 1870 resulted in a renewed interest in the northern mountains. By this time a considerable number of prospectors and miners were arriving in Montana. Many of them were seeking new fields, apart from the gold and copper mining regions of Butte and Anaconda. The first recorded party of miners to enter the area was one headed by Frank Lehman who in 1870 came up the Flathead over Marias Pass and onto the prairies into what is now Alberta, on an unsuccessful mining venture. About the same time a minor gold stampede, also doomed to failure, brought other miners through Marias Pass and sent them back disappointed.

The next account of miners entering the region was in 1876 when a party of Texans was reported to have entered the park on a prospecting trip. This account related in a letter by one of the participants many years later, had not been verified by any other source, so the dates may or may not be exactly correct. This letter, written by one William Veach, concerns a prospecting trip taken by himself, Emerson Brown, Thomas Molenieux, a man known as Crow, and one other. They drifted north through Colorado, Wyoming and eastern Montana. After spending several days in the vicinity of St. Mary Lake, they crossed Logan Pass, dropped down past Lake McDonald and went on to Belton where they picked up some supplies. This is believed to be the first recorded trip of white men over Logan Pass.

From Belton the party went up the North Fork of the Flathead and eventually reached Quartz Lake, where they built a cabin on the northeast corner of the lake and are reported to have found a 30-ounce nugget of gold in the creek flowing into the lake. In September, Veach and one other left for California and did not return, so we have no further record of what happened to the remainder of the party or their 30-ounce nugget.

In the late 1880's there occurred a short-lived mining boom at the headwaters of Mineral Creek. Mrs. Nat Collins, popularly known as the "Cattle Queen of Montana," hired a crew of men and set up a camp on a small stream feeding Mineral Creek, in the upper McDonald Valley, to develop a supposedly rich prospect there. With Mrs. Collins acting as both foreman and cook, they worked the mine for three summers and one winter. After finding no rich mineral deposits, she finally sent to St. Paul for a mining engineer to look the mine over and he advised her to drop the venture and stop wasting her money. The crew then shifted to Columbia Falls to cut ties for the Great Northern Railway, and Mrs. Collins returned to her ranch at Choteau, Montana. The stream upon which the mine was located is still known as "Cattle Queen Creek."

Until 1890 prospecting in the area was somewhat aimless and spasmodic. Then, from 1890 to 1893 reports began to sift out and circulate in the mining areas of Butte and Anaconda that there were rich veins of copper ore to be found in these mountains. As a result, prospectors began to flock to them. One such report that appeared in the Fort Benton "River Press" stated that a prospector named "Dutch Lui" had struck a vein at the head of Copper and Quartz Creeks carrying gold, silver, copper and lead, assaying from $80 to $500 per ton.

Ceded Strips

Although prospecting was carried on quite feverishly through the mountains, the area east of the Continental Divide was Indian Reservation and as such was legally closed to all entry for prospecting purposes. The fact that the area was closed was enough to fire the imagination of miners throughout the state, and tales of great wealth in these hills began to circulate through he country. The cry soon arose that the government had "locked up" the area o prevent the taking of these minerals. This, in turn, interested more miners,

36

and pressure was put upon Congress to throw the region open to mining. In the meantime, the more adventurous prospectors were sneaking into the area and bringing out stories that tended to further feed the fire.

As the pressure increased, Congress could no longer ignore it. In 1895 William C. Pollock, George Bird Grinnell and Walter M. Clements were appointed as a commission of three to negotiate with the Blackfeet for the purchase of the strip of land lying between the Continental Divide and the prairies, from Canada south some fifty or sixty miles. After long negotiations, they finally agreed on a purchase price of $1,500,000, which they recommended to Congress. The Indians retained the right to hunt, fish and cut timber on this area, soon to be known as the "Ceded Strip," unless the State of Montana should at some time deem it unlawful. The area of the strip included the eastern part of what is now Glacier National Park and Portions of the Lewis and Clark National Forest immediately south of the park. That portion now included within Glacier National Park was withdrawn from hunting and timber cutting provisions of the treaty with the establishment of the park in 1910.

On June 10, 1896, Congress confirmed the purchase of the Ceded Strip from the Blackfeet for the price agreed upon by the commissioners, but the land was still not legally opened for mining until 1898. In the meantime, miners and prospectors, often called "sooners," began to sneak in and locate claims in preparation for the day when they could come in legally and occupy them.

Swiftcurrent Mining Boom

The years of 1898 to 1900 constituted the hey-day of the short-lived mining excitement in the park. On April 15, 1898, the "Ceded Strip" was thrown open to miners and settlers. Great tales of mineral wealth had come out of the area and small veins of mineral ore had actually been discovered in the Swiftcurrent Valley and other localities throughout the park area. Throughout the entire period however, the Swiftcurrent Valley constituted the major attraction for the miners and contained the bulk of the claims and activity. Frank Stevenson, an early prospector and settler in the valley, tells of guiding the soldiers into the Swiftcurrent area to control the opening of the Strip. On the appointed day and hour, a volley of shots rang out and the rush was on—a wild stampede of miners on horses, in wagons, and even on foot. Within a matter of hours hundreds of claims were staked in the Swiftcurrent Valley and adjacent mountains. Stevenson himself staked several claims, some of which later yielded showings of oil and a mill site and water rights at Swiftcurrent Falls.

The mining boom in the Swiftcurrent Valley was very active for several years, but as little or no minerals were found where there was thought to have been a bonanza, interest died and the flurry of activity gradually ceased. By 1903 most of the claims were abandoned except for the more persistent miners, many of whom held on until the time of their deaths. This short-lived boom though, did produce several interesting developments, principally in the field of finance and promotion. The size and scope of the promotional activity was sometimes startling. Companies were formed and capitalized at hundreds of thousands of shares; a town sprang up in the area almost overnight and as rapidly disappeared; an entire stamp mill and reduction plant was transported into the far reaches of Canyon Creek. These and many similar items make this one of the most interesting periods in Glacier's history.

A good example of the lengths men will go to in the hopes of realizing a fortune from the elusive mineral leads is evident in the story of the Cracker Lake Mine. "On April 12, 1898, just three days before the official opening of the Ceded Strip, a mine was located on the so-called Cracker Lead, on the shore of Cracker Lake at the extreme head of the steep, narrow Canyon Creek Valley. Following the official opening of the area, work commenced on the lead and soon samples of ore were taken out to show prospective investors. Many theories have been advanced as to where these rich samples originated, as the mine never did produce paying ore in any quantity and not one pound was ever taken out of it commercially. Yet the investors were interested and sufficient capital was raised to develop the mine properly. The area soon became a beehive of activity as the shaft was driven farther and farther into the mountain, finally reaching a length of well over 1,300 feet. In the meantime work was started on a 100-ton concentrator to be located on the shore of Cracker Lake. The mill was hauled in and installed but never turned a wheel, and its remains can still be seen near the old mine entrance." [25]

Charles Nielson, of East Glacier Park, recalls the difficulties involved in transporting the 16,000 pound concentrator from Fort Browning to the mine. He used a large freight wagon and twelve head of husky mules on the 29-day trip to the mine. There was very little road on the way and none after leaving the Swiftcurrent Valley. Often the load was hauled with block and tackle up the bed of Canyon Creek. Upon looking at this valley today, one can but wonder at the work and perseverance exhibited by Nielson as he toiled up this narrow gorge with his staggering load—and at the contracted rate of twenty-five dollars per day.

In March of 1901, the Cracker Jack and Bulls Head mines, the latter on the slopes of Mt. Wilbur, were consolidated into the "Michigan and Montana Company," which was capitalized at $300,000. In spite of this backing though, by 1902 the mining activity dropped off, along with that of many other mines in the area. Some interest was kept alive in the mine for a number of years, but little or no work was done and all that remains today is a caved in tunnel and a pile of steel and old lumber on the site of the mill.

The land containing the Cracker Lake and Bulls Head mines changed hands several time in the years to follow and was finally picked up on a tax deed from Glacier County on September 22, 1953 by the Glacier Natural History Association. In October of 1953, the land was turned over to the Federal Government for $123.96, the cost of acquiring it and clearing title. Thus ended the story of the largest and perhaps the most famous of the mining ventures in Glacier National Park.

FORMER TOWN OF ALTYN

Coincident with and mainly due to the development of the Cracker Lake Mine, a small boom town sprang up at the mouth of Canyon Creek near the head of Sherburne Lake. This town, named Altyn, after Dave Greenwood Altyn, one of the backers of the Cracker Jack, continued as the center of activity for the valley as long as the mining activity existed. At its height this busy little "metropolis" contained a dozen or so buildings, including a post office, a store, several saloons and dance halls, a two-story hotel building, and a few tent-houses and cabins that served as residences. The years of 1899 and 1900 saw the height of this town, after which it dropped rapidly into obscurity; all that remains today are a few excavations along the shore of Sherburne Lake on what is known as "Cracker Flats."

Most of the mining claims were soon abandoned, but several were worked quite extensively and patented, granting permanent ownership to the claimant. Although few are still in private hands within the park, most have been bought by the Federal Government or are in the process of being acquired.

The Search for Oil

The other phase of the mineral activity in the park was that of the oil boom, at about the same time as the mining boom or shortly thereafter. Coincident with the opening of the eastern slopes of the mountains to mining was the discovery of oil seepage at the head of Kintla Lake on the western slopes. Here prospectors discovered oil seeping out in the water of a spring at the foot of what was then known as Forum Peak. This discovery led to considerable excitement around Butte; a man by the name of Bender formed an oil company and set out to locate a road to Kintla Lake in order that he might haul drilling equipment to the lake. In the summer of 1901, the newly formed Butte Oil Company put crews to work cutting out a road from the foot of Lake McDonald to the site of their oil well at the upper end of Kintla Lake. The resultant stretch of road, about forty miles in length, could hardly be called a road by present standards, since it consisted merely of a route cut through the timber, with corduroy laid over the swampy areas. No grading was done nor were there any bridges built. But in spite of this, most of the heavy machinery and supplies were hauled in before snow fell that fall. After the lake froze that winter, and when the machinery was hauled to the head of the lake over the ice, drilling was started and continued for several years. When no traces of oil were found, however, the well was abandoned and the Butte Oil Well joined the ranks of those forgotten mines and wells of which little remains today except a hole in the ground and a few bits of rotted timber and rusted iron.

Kintla Lake Oil Well

About the same time the Kintla Well was drilled on the North Fork. This well was located near the river, not far from the mouth of Kintla Creek and, like the Butte Well, did not produce and was finally abandoned.

The biggest oil boom in the park area, oddly enough, occurred in the same valley as did the largest mining boom—Swiftcurrent Valley. Credit for the discovery of oil in this valley seems to go to Sam Somes who ran the hotel at the town of Altyn. Sam evidently had some claims in the lower valley, near the site of the present Sherburne Dam, and one day in 1901, while he was doing assessment work in his tunnel following a dynamite charge, he discovered small pools of oil on the floor of the tunnel. As he worked on into the tunnel he continued to find traces of this oil seepage. This interested him and he collected some samples of the oil and headed for Great Falls where he talked

Old Well, Kintla Lake Oil Well. 1904.

KINTLA LAKE OIL WELL

to some friends about it. As a result, the Montana Swiftcurrent Oil Company was organized, with Somes as general manager, and was capitalized at $1,500,000.00

Equipment and men were soon organized and moved to the drilling site. Drilling operations were started and continued through the spring and summer of 1903, at which time Somes, to create more interest in the venture, took a bottle of oil to Great Falls and persisted in pouring it on the floors and desks in the banks and offices around town. The result of this little performance was the formation of several oil companies and the resultant grabbing up of practically all the land on the floor of Swiftcurrent Valley, along with some in adjacent valleys, for "oil-placer" claims.

Somes' well never did produce either gas or oil, although a few of the others produced gas in varying quantities and some even showed traces of oil, none of it in commercial quantities. The only claim this company has to fame is the fact that it was the discovery well and the first oil well drilled on the eastern side of the park.

By the fall of 1903, most of the miners were gone from the valley, and many of the oil-placer claims were abandoned, but during the summer Mike

Cassidy, one of the prospectors, had observed bubbles arising from the waters of a small creek emptying into Sherburne Lake. This, coupled with Somes' discovery in 1901 made him suspicious of the possibility of oil there. He immediately got busy and before long another oil company, one that was to make its mark on the history of the valley, sprang into existence. The Cassidy-Swiftcurrent Oil Company, under manager and driller Matt Dunn, started drilling on what was known as St. Louis Placer No. 1. In 1905 and 1906 gas was struck; drilling continued intermittently until 1909, when tools were lost in the hole. Cassidy spent the next three summers in an unsuccessful attempt to retrieve them. No oil was struck in this well although gas was found on three levels. In 1907, Cassidy piped the gas from the well to his house and used it until 1914 for heating and lighting.

When plans were made to construct the Sherburne Reservoir, condemnation proceedings were directed against the portion of this claim that was below the flowage level of the proposed reservoir. On August 28, 1920, this claim was settled with the Federal Government paying Cassidy the sum of $7,675.00 for that part of the claim below the flow line, which included the gas well. Later Cassidy exchanged the remaining acreage for lands outside the park.

The largest and probably the most controversial of all the oil companies to arise at this time was the Swift Current Oil Land and Power Company, incorporated on April 30, 1904. The original incorporators were J. H. Sherburne of Browning, Dave Greenwood Altyn, for whom the town of Altyn had been named, F. M. Stevenson who had a cabin and a claim nearby, A. J. Gibson of Missoula, Otto J. Hartwig of Chicago and Sherburne Morse of Browning. Many of the claim-holders up and down the valley soon assigned their claims to the new company in return for shares; and through this the company acquired twenty-nine claims totaling approximately four thousand acres of land, and was capitalized at two million shares.

A professional driller was imported from West Virginia and paid $80 per month and board. Drilling was intermittent and slow, and continued until 1907, after which the machinery was loaned to another company and all work on the well ceased. Two wells were drilled by the company, only one of which produced any oil, and that in very small quantities. This well went down to a depth of 1,500 feet and cost, in cash, $19,900, plus what was paid out in shares.

The most interesting thing about this well was the fact that in 1905 a diploma was awarded to the Swift Current Oil Land and Power Company, reading in part: "Awarded to Swift Current Oil Land and Power Company for the first producing oil well in the State of Montana, and the best display of crude and refined oil from the Swift Current District, Teton County, Montana, at the State Fair, Helena, Montana, 1905." As very little oil was ever produced from this well, there persisted the ever-present rumor that the company imported barrels of crude oil and poured them into the well to "grease" the investors, while others maintained that the well was an actual, bonafide producer. In any event, it received the fame and the certificate, and must have produced some oil in order to have done so.

The oil boom died out almost completely after 1907, except for a few oil men, like the few remaining miners, who could not give up the idea of finding a million dollars that all the others had overlooked. A few more holes were drilled, but nothing except a trace here and there was ever found. Frank Stevenson, who remained to make his home in the valley, gradually came into possession of some of the more promising claims, including some that he had staked himself; he built his home on one of them, where he lived for many years, spending some time as a park ranger when the area was first included in Glacier National Park.

Galbraith's map of June 1923, shows that the entire valley floor from the vicinity of the Sherburne Dam to Swiftcurrent Falls was taken up at one time by these oil placer claims. In all, between eight and ten wells were drilled in the valley, mostly near the valley floor and within two miles of the present Sherburne Dam. The waters of the Sherburne Reservoir now cover most of the old well sites.

Mapping of the Park

Concurrent with the mining activity in the park, came a desire for more accurate maps of the area, and the Geological Survey sent crews into the area, starting in 1900, to map the park and the adjacent mountains. This project was carried on through the years 1900 to 1904, and the maps that resulted were so well done and accurate that they are still used today as the official maps of the area. F. E. Matthes, R. H. Chapman, and other old topographers who worked on this project did a job of mapping that is still talked about by topographers the world over. During the summer of 1901, the Survey also sent in geologists Bailey Willis and George Finlay, along with paleontologist Stuart Weller, to make a geological study of the area and Dr. Willis at this time described and named the famous Lewis Overthrust.

Before we leave the mining days mention should be made of the ill-fated voyage of the steamer "Oakes" up the North Fork of the Flathead River in an attempt to haul coal from deposits near the mouth of Logging Creek. About the time that the Great Northern Railway came through the area, coal was discovered along the western bank of the North Fork, not far from Logging Creek.

VOYAGE OF THE STEAMER "OAKES"

"Rusting away on a gravel bed under the west end of the bridge a quarter mile below the southwest corner of Glacier National Park lies an old steam boiler. For almost half a century it has lain there, abandoned, isolated and almost forgotten. The building of the new bridge across the Flathead at that point last summer has broken its long isolation. It is not much to see, but it is a relic of an enterprise, probably the most romantic and adventurous in the development of northwestern Montana, the ill-starred voyage of the steamer 'Oakes.'

Some time previous to 1890 important coal deposits had been discovered far up the North Fork of the Flathead River. Near the same time James A. Talbott, an enterprising character who had prospered in the rush days of the Butte mining development came into the Flathead country. With others he acquired the townsite of Columbia Falls ahead of the railroad and built a palatial home on the bank of the river nearby.

Talbott was a man of considerable vision, and in those days was able to back his dreams with tangible substance. He learned of the coal deposits on the North Fork and conceived the idea of using this coal to induce the construction of a railroad into that region, which would bless his town of Columbia Falls and would greatly stimulate the development of the whole region.

But many miles of the most difficult terrain in the state covered with an almost impenetrable jungle of virgin forest lay between the townsite and the prospective mines. When the Great Northern, building westward, reached Columbia Falls, Talbott decided on a desperate effort to bring out a carload sample of that North Fork coal. He recognized the practical impossibility of over-land transportation and knowing full well the hazardous nature of the enterprise, had a steamboat built at a cost of above five thousand dollars to attempt the navigation of the swift and turbulent river.

This steamer, named The Oakes, was a stern wheeler about seventy-five feet long and fairly broad of beam, carried a power winch on the forward deck in anticipation of the need of extra power in the swift and almost continuous rapids up-stream.

The Oakes was captained and piloted by two experienced river men, Steve Lereau and Christian Prestbye, supported by a crew of a dozen or so hardy and resourceful men. The engine was operated by a man named Doyle; the boiler was fired by a husky youth, Claude Slemmer. Riggers for handling towlines and shore gear included Mike Shannon, Bob Hunter, Tom MacDonald, and a tall and wiry youngster remembered only as Slim. An old man of sixty-five years, probably a crony of Talbott's earlier days at Butte, was one of the crew, and Talbott himself, never asking any man to do what he would not try himself, was a useful man on board.

Any casual fisherman who has fished on the Flathead through and above Bad Rock Canyon and along the tortuous, rockribbed channel of the North Fork with its rapids, shoals and whirling pools at low water, would marvel

44

that the attempt at navigation was ever made. Looking down now from the North Fork Road high above the narrow, crooked ribbon of black, green and white water which zig-zags between boulders and projecting rocks at mid-summer, it is appalling to think of the hazards threatening a ship like the Oakes which must make the attempt in the swift, gray, swirling flood of snow water of the spring thaws.

But early in May, 1892, The Oakes and its daring crew steamed away from its moorings at Columbia Falls and headed up the swollen flood of the Flathead River. Hopes were high and the start was auspicious. Talbott's enthusiasm inspired the crew and all were in a holiday humor. Their whistle blasts awoke the echoes as they steamed up through Bad Rock Canyon, passed the mouth of the South Fork, carefully threaded the narrower swifter waters of the Baby Canyon, and swung away to the north. Fortune still smiled as the stern-wheel threshed the swift gray waters and they moved slowly but stubbornly up stream. They passed beneath the high bridge of the Great Northern at the site of the present town of Coram and onward, without incident, to the foot of the Red Lick rapids some three miles beyond.

There was the first stern crisis of the voyage. Slemmer fired the boiler to the limit of its capacity and Doyle nursed the engine with the available steam while Prestbye steered to keep an open channel and to meet the merciless current from the most favorable angles. They almost reached the comparatively quiet waters above the rapids when, short of steam, the plucky engine faltered and The Oakes lost headway and drifted almost helpless in the racing water.

It was their first moment of extreme peril. A small boat was carried for a tender. Mike Shannon and Bob Hunter quickly launched this boat and rowed ashore in desperate haste with a tow line. A single turn of the line around the nearest tree, a half-formed knot, and a quick haul by the power winch and The Oakes and her crew were first saved from going broadside down the rocky channel.

Their predicament now demonstrated the necessity of more rope. A single tow-line was not enough. There were many such rapids ahead and on most of them a cross-haul would be required to hold The Oakes in mid-stream while the winch and the main tow-line furnished the forward power. The Oakes and her crew were forced to remain moored at the Red Licks while the husky and boatwise young Slemmer took the small boat and went back down stream to Columbia Falls for more rope.

Slemmer narrowly missed death when a veritable maelstrom opened before him as he rounded a projecting rock in the canyon on the way to town and he decided it was folly to return upstream with the heavy rope in the small boat; so he got aboard a freight train with his rope and with the magic of Tal-

45

bott's name induced the crew to let him off at the nearest point to the tethered Oakes and her impatiently waiting crew.

There was now no small boat for a tender and from this point on there was almost constant need for a shore crew on the other shore to rig the cross-haul which, in the absence of a second winch, was operated by a hasty improvisation they referred to as a Spanish windlass crudely constructed when and where needed on shore. Shannon and Hunter usually manned the main tow-line while Slemmer and Slim rigged the cross-haul and the rest did their share of the strenuous work on board.

They passed the mouth of the Middle Fork and by slow and difficult stages worked on northward into the ever narrowing and quickening current of the North Fork. They were now shut in on all sides by absolutely primitive wilderness. To their right lay the wild and fequently perpendicular jungle which would one day be Glacier National Park, while on the left lay the almost equally rugged foothills of the Whitefish Mountains. Nature has seldom locked more securely her treasure-house than she locked the gate to her North Fork coal.

It was good game country and frequently deer and moose appeared on the river banks and once seven deer were seen swimming across the river up stream. The animals had a hard struggle and were excited by the strange monster snorting in the river below them. They reached the bank at a precipitous spot and, well spent from their effort, again and again they scrambled madly to scale the rocks and fell back splashing into the water. Young Slemmer seized his rifle to try for some venison but Talbott shouted, "They've earned their lives," and dissuaded him.

Just below the mouth of Canyon Creek, The Oakes was swept out of the main channel and caught in a broad whirling pool where she milled round and round with a mass of logs and brush in a situation which bid fair to be the end of her. After much hazardous maneuvering the two lines were rigged and the boat was again worked into the stream. When she finally swung into the channel and started forward, Slemmer's hold on the Spanish windlass slipped and it spun like a deadly pin-wheel over his head as he ducked and the line and windlass were dragged away into the river.

Many days had passed and they were less than fifteen miles from their starting point. The current was growing more turbulent and the channel more dangerous every mile. It had been a precarious venture from the start. But these men were pioneers and had the crazy persistence of their kind. By this time they must have realized the futility of the enterprise but they did not turn back.

Two or three miles above Canyon Creek the last line was put ashore. Shannon and Hunter snubbed it to the only tree strategically located and the winch began to haul. The Oakes rolled and yawed from side to side of the

46

channel and rocked dangerously as the turbulent water struck it from different angles. From the rigorous strains of the voyage The Oakes was taking some water in the hold, and this, set in motion, added to the instability of the craft. Now on a particularly violent yaw she finally capsized near the east bank and began slowly to turn over. The added pull of the capsized boat was too much for the tree which held the line. It was pulled out by the roots and both boat and tree drifted down the stream.

Most of the crew scrambled ashore on the east shore in this final catastrophe, Christian Prestbye climbed through the window of the pilot house as the water rushed in at the door. Talbott and two other men were not so fortunate. They had, however, been able to scramble up the side as she turned over and were still on top when she floated into midstream and finally grounded nearly bottom up on a gravel bar some distance below.

The situation of these three men was now critical. The boat might roll at any moment. No man could swim that icy flood. Those on shore were without tools. They had a length of rope but too short to reach the wreck. In this emergency they siezed a dead, half-rotted fir tree and by strength of many hands broke it in many pieces. They stranded the rope and constructed a crude raft which they let float down towards the wreck at the end of the spliced strands. After many unsuccessful efforts they maneuvered this raft near enough to The Oakes for one of the men to get aboard and he was hauled ashore. Three times the operation was repeated and all were finally on firm land.

The steamer Oakes had made her first and last voyage and in this effort it became the only steam driven boat ever operated on the Flathead or its branches above Kalispell.

But the crew of The Oakes was in a sorry plight; not a single axe, not an ounce of food, not a single match in all the company. Talbott alone had been able to salvage a single wet blanket. All were soaked to the skin. The snows of winter still lingered in the deep woods and the temperature at night dropped well below the freezing point. From the other bank a blazed trail was known to Columbia Falls while many miles of unmarked and well-nigh impassable wilderness intervened on any other avenue of escape.

In this dilemma Claude Slemmer suggested crossing the river on crude rafts such as they had used to rescue the three men from the wreck. Only Slim would agree to such a venture. So Slemmer and Slim, on the raft of rotten fir, with only a rough pole and a piece of broken board from the wreck to work with, set out to cross the swift gray flood while the rest of the hungry, shivering crew stood on the shore and watched them drift out of sight. To traverse the difficult terrain which lay between the larger group and their nearest contact with civilization, the railroad station at Belton, would have been sufficiently strenuous in their condition if the hills had been bare and the visibility good, but with those tumbled hills and ravines deep clad in a tangled jungle of primeval forest the task was formidable indeed.

One man of the party professed to know of a short cut across country and most of the men, including Talbott, chose to follow his lead. Tom Mac-Donald, who had injured an ankle in the mad scramble ashore, and the old gentleman from Butte, preferred to keep the river in sight, work down the North Fork to its confluence with the Middle Fork and then up that stream towards Belton. Mike Shannon, feeling that these men needed an able companion, accompanied them on their longer but more reliable course.

The two groups separated. The dreary chilly day was passing. A few hours later and a couple of miles down stream Shannon heard distant voices. After some hallooing back and forth the two parties were together again. The overland party had become confused in the maze of hills and tangled forest, lost its bearing, and blindly circled to the river again.

Night came, cold and cheerless. They bedded themselves the best they could and all lay down to sleep except the old fellow from Butte. He paced a beat all night, stamping his feet and threshing his arms to keep the blood in circulation and occasionally kicking the others awake lest they die of chill in their sleep. But they had huddled well together and all were able to chatter their teeth in the morning.

There was no breakfast to get and no dishes to wash so they were on their way early, separated as before. The larger group was still hopeful of finding a short way through but in a few hours bewilderment and blind circling brought them again to the river bank and reunion with Shannon and his companions. Together they tramped on, up hill and down, over rocks and through quagmire, drenched and switched by the dripping brush and branches, tripped by lopping brambles and creeping vines and clawed and scratched by devil's clubs till it seemed that the old demon himself was belaboring them. And while these tortures beset from without, hunger was boring from within.

Eventually game and Indian trails brought them to a deserted Indian camp for another cold and cheerless night and early the next morning they came out on the bank of McDonald Creek.

The creek was bank full and cold enough to rattle. But there, a hundred feet away, tugging at its moorings on the other bank, was a small scow. 'How much is that boat worth, Jim,' someone asked of Talbott. 'Five thousand dollars,' shouted Talbott and probably meant it. But money was not an object now, only a word of jest. All hands combined to break down small trees and to weave them into a sort of matlike raft which when done was little more than a brush pile. On this floating brush pile Mike Shannon made a precarious crossing and secured that precious scow.

Shannon and Bob Hunter ferried the wretched party across McDonald Creek one at a time and not long after used the same small scow likewise in crossing the foaming waters of the Middle Fork a mile or so below Belton.

When the famished party had finally straggled into Belton Station and had secured some food, they Missed Tom MacDonald and the old gentleman from Butte. Shannon and Hunter, the strongest of the weary group, took food and retraced their steps. They found the missing men, exhausted and bewildered, just off the trail on the last mile.

With a little aid, these men finally reached the station and with all accounted for Talbott telegraphed for a dead-head special which returned them to Columbia Falls.

In the meantime wreckage from The Oakes had floated away down the river and had been observed from the river bank near town. The catastrophe was confirmed when a board bearing the broad lettered name floated beneath the bridge and past the Talbott mansion on the bank nearby.

A rescue party was speedily organized and started on the woods trail north.

Returning to Slemmer and Slim adrift on the turbulent North Fork, poling and paddling frantically to cross the swift seething current on the rotten and waterlogged raft, their progress downstream was rapid but across channel was painfully slow. When they neared the west bank, Slim's pole was caught between submerged rocks and twisted from his grasp. Slemmer paddled furiously with his broken board while Slim made more or less futile grabs at the tops of submerged bushes in efforts to push towards shore. Below there loomed the broad whirl where The Oakes had milled around and their situation was growing more desperate second by second when Slim with long arm outstretched, at last gained a precious hold and they swung ashore.

Some distance farther down stream they were fortunate enough to find part of an abandoned lunch in very good condition, left by some hardy wanderer. They devoured it and went on. Soon after they found the dim trail which led to Columbia Falls and suffered no further hardship. A few miles from town they met the rescue party which on learning the whereabouts of the rest of the crew returned with them to town.

Such was the the story of a glorious adventure but to these men it was only a work-a-day affair. Not one of them thought it worth while to write any account of it. Jim Talbott is dead these many years. And of that lusty crew only two are known to be alive, Mike Shannon of Glacier Park Station and Claude Slemmer of Kalispell. To these two, now aged but still colorful oldtimers the writer of this tale is indebted for the facts of this romantic adventure.

The writer had heard fragmentary accounts of this ill-starred venture for years, and feeling that the account of such constructive exploits deserves a place in the history of our state as surely as the lawless forays of Henry Plummer and his gang, he has interviewed Shannon and Slemmer and the resultant story is as true as the memories of the two aged survivors.

When the flood waters of that season had subsided, blankets, tools and wreckage littered the stream bed and decorated the bushes and rocks for miles below the point of tragedy. Later Shannon salvaged the winch, added a gas engine for power and used it successfully as a stump puller for several years. Others salvaged the boiler from where it had dropped from the over-turned wreck and attempted to bring it out on a raft, but the raft was wrecked and the boiler finally came to rest on a gravel bar just below the mouth of the Middle Fork where it has lain half buried in the gravel for nearly half a century. Fishermen have reported seeing the engine in the bottom of a deep pool near the mouth of Canyon Creek. Slemmer's rifle was never found, and the old hulk eventually drifted away to parts unknown. Thus The Steamer Oakes and this episode of daily life has become an epic of the pioneers.

A year later, again under the auspices of Talbott, Shannon and five men constructed a huge raft at the mine site and actually brought out half a car load of coal. In an effort to repeat the exploit the second raft was wrecked, the crew deserted, and Mike was compelled to give up the enterprise." [26]

Ironically, when a road was finally opened up to these coal banks and production started, the coal was found to be of such low grade that it was un-economical to continue to work them and the mine was soon closed down.

CHAPTER II

National Park Movement

EARLY LAND WITHDRAWALS

We are more or less familiar with the history of forest conservation in the United States—how the forests were stripped from one region after another, until a few far-sighted men began to wonder what was to happen when all these areas were denuded, and decided to do something about it. The result was a demand for withdrawal of certain forested areas from un-regulated public entry and the wholesale cutting of timber. This movement, indirectly, led to the establishment of Glacier National Park.

The first effort towards withdrawal of the lands included in the park occurred in 1885, when a bill was introduced into the Senate of the United States "To establish a Forest Reservation on the headwaters of the Missouri River and headwaters of the Clark's Fork of the Columbia River." The bill evidently did not go far, but it did start a movement ending in the setting aside of the forested areas in the northern Rocky Mountains; for on March 3, 1891, Congress passed an act authorizing the president to set aside forest reserves in the forested lands of the nation, to be administered by the Department of the Interior. This area in western Montana was designated as a forest reserve but little was done with it until 1897.

On February 22 of that year, largely through the initiative of the United States Forest Commission, of which Charles S. Sargent was chairman, the Lewis and Clark Forest Reserve was formed. This reserve included all of what is now Glacier National Park, the Kootenai, Blackfeet, Flathead, and Lewis and Clark National Forests, that portion north of the Great Northern Railroad being called the North Division and that south of the railroad, the South Division.

With the formation of the Forest Reserves also came the demand for personnel to administer and protect them, and in 1900 President Theodore Roosevelt appointed one of his former "Rough Riders," Frank Herrig, as forest ranger to patrol the country drained by the North Fork of the Flathead River. As far as the records show, Herrig was the first Federal officer

FRANK LIEBIG

51

to be placed in charge of any area included in the park. Those who knew Herrig described him as an imposing figure who generally rode a big bay horse, decked out with a silver-mounted bridle and martingale. He wore high-topped boots, a big "44" strapped on his belt and a 45-70 rifle in a scabbard on his saddle. He always wore his large ranger's badge in plain sight, and his constant companion was a large Russian wolfhound.

Frank Liebig

The next forest ranger to be appointed to the park area was Frank Liebig, who was appointed on June 1, 1902, for the district that included what is now all of the north end of Glacier National Park. He was assigned to "look for fires, timber thieves, which were plentiful along the Great Northern Railway, and to look for squatters and game violators." [27] When given his badge by the Forest Supervisor, along with a double-bitted axe, a crosscut saw and a box of ammunition for his rifle, he was told to "Go to it and good luck. The whole country is yours, from Belton to Canada and across the Rockies to the prairie or Waterton Lake and the foot of St. Mary Lake." [28] Operating out of his ranger station at the head of Lake McDonald, Liebig remained in sole charge of the entire area, until the time it was made a park in 1910. His hobby was bird taxidermy and the best of his work during that time is now a part of the Glacier National Park collection.

LAKE McDONALD RANGER STATION—1905

Lake McDonald Ranger Station — in 1905

In 1905 the Forest Reserves were taken out of the Department of the Interior and the Forest Service was set up under the Department of Agriculture. With the establishment in 1910, of Glacier National Park the Forest Service again turned this area of some 1,500 square miles back to the Department of the Interior in whose hands it has since remained.

ESTABLISHMENT OF THE PARK

When we think about the origin of areas such as this and other National Parks, we naturally ask the question, "When did this park idea originate, and who was responsible for it?" Often this question is hard to answer because we do not know the thoughts that may have run through the minds of the early explorers and travelers, but we do have written records of the ideas of these men.

Action toward Establishment of the Park

Contrary to the general belief that George Bird Grinnell first thought of this as a national park, we have the record in the Fort Benton "River Press" in 1883, of a letter from Lieutenant John T. Van Orsdale in which he makes the following statement: "I sincerely hope that publicity now being given to that portion of Montana will result in drawing attention to the scenery which surpasses anything in Montana or adjacent territories. A great benefit would result to Montana if this section could be set aside as a national park . . ." In this letter he was referring to the area that is now included in the park and through which he and Lieutenant Woodruff traveled some ten years before.

George Bird Grinnell, at that time editor of the magazine "Forest and Stream," first came to the area of the park in 1885 and again in 1887, and thereafter almost yearly as long as he was able. To Grinnell goes the credit, and justly so, for swinging public opinion in favor of making this area into a national park, and also for promoting the legislation that made it possible. During his visits in 1885 and 1887 he explored the St. Mary and Swiftcurrent Valleys and named many of the features within them. It must have been during these trips that he began to formulate his own ideas of what should become of the area, for it was while on one of his trips into the upper reaches of the St. Mary Valley in 1891 that he made an entry in his notebook to the effect that this area should become a national park. And what is more, he immediately set about to do something about it.

Grinnell's first public attempt to do this was through an article in the "Century Magazine" of September, 1901, entitled, "The Crown of the Continent," in which he described in glowing terms the beauties of the area and suggested that a movement be started to set aside the area around St. Mary Lake as a National Park.

Grinnell then went a step further and was instrumental in getting the noted writer, Emerson Hough, to come to the area and write a series of articles for "Forest and Stream" magazine. Hough made two trips to the area in 1902, one in February and one in August, both times guided into the back country by James Willard Schultz, who was also sending articles to Grinnell.

These articles created considerable interest in the area, and the local, and some national, newspapers began to take it up. Finally, through pressure exerted by Grinnell and others, the necessary legislation was drawn up and the Congressional mill began to grind.

Legislative History of Establishment

The actual start of legislative action to form Glacier National Park took place on December 11, 1907, when United States Senator T. H. Carter of

Montana introduced a bill into the Senate to set aside the area as a national park. The bill being considered by the Senate was found to have several undesirable clauses in it and the bill was sent back to Carter for rewriting.

Senator Carter immediately revised the bill as suggested and again presented it to the Senate on February 24, 1908. The Committee on Public Lands approved the bill, with amendments, and it was sent to the floor of the Senate where it was approved and passed. On May 16, it was then sent to the House of Representatives, where Congressman Charles N. Pray, Montana's only member of the House, took it under his wing and guided it through the Committee on Public Lands, of which he was a member. Although this committee reported it back to the House with the recommendation that it be passed as amended by the Senate, no action was taken on it and the bill died.

On June 26, 1909, Carter introduced the bill to the Senate for the third time. This time it lay in the Public Lands Committee until January 25, 1910, when it was reported out by Senator Dixon of Montana. It was brought up on the floor of the Senate and agreed to on February 9. From there it again went to the House of Representatives, where it was finally agreed to with further amendments. Taking the lead, Congressman Pray, along with several other members, fought very strongly to get the bill through the House.

The Senate then objected to the amendments written in by the House, and a Conference Committee was appointed to iron out the differences. The committee reached a compromise and the bill was again presented to the House and agreed to without a record vote. On the same day it was presented to the Senate, who also agreed to it. From there the bill went to President Taft who affixed his signature to it on May 11, 1910, bringing Glacier National Park into existence.

Ten days after the approval of the bill, on May 21, 1910, the first appropriation for Glacier National Park was presented to the Senate, and approved as part of the Sundry Civil Appropriations Act for the fiscal year 1911, approved on June 25. This Act carried an item, "For improvement of Glacier National Park, Montana, for construction of trails and roads, $50,000." Glacier National Park was on its own.

It is interesting to note the opposition to the bill to establish the park. Grazing and lumber interests, the ones that would seem most likely to object, showed little interest in it. Mining activity had almost completely died out, so there was little objection there. But certain local groups, mainly from Kalispell, cried out loud and long that it was a scheme of the Great Northern Railway to prevent other roads from entering the region. Their contention was that the railroad had persuaded Senator Carter to put up the bill so that no other railroads could use the passes to the north of them not realizing, of course, that there were no passes to the north that were suitable for a railroad to use. The truth of the matter was that the late Louis W. Hill, Sr., then president of the Great Northern, was foremost among the sponsors of the bill, hoping with Senator Carter, Congressman Pray, George Bird Grinnell and others to create a public recreational area for Montana which would attract tourists and subsequently a source of passenger traffic and new income dollars for the state. Opposition also came from legislators who contended that it was not the function of the government to dabble in recreation.

After passage of the bill seemed certain the opposition interests began to back track and explain their reasons for it. The following excerpt from an editorial in the Kalispell Daily Inter Lake attempted to clarify their stand on the matter: "The establishment of the park is not a calamity. The original opposition was due mainly to personal interests, such as a loss of hunting grounds, locking up of the area, no settling on the North Fork, etc." There was much 'to do' about it until the bill was changed to suit the people. One principal fear was of military control.

Regarding the final passage of this bill in the House of Representatives, Congressman Pray is reported to have made the statement that one of the biggest helps he had in getting the bill through was the weather. It was so extremely hot that day that many of the Congressmen were not present and Pray, who was instrumental in guiding it through the house, was able to muster enough supporters to pass it on the floor, or at least bring the remainder around to his way of thinking.

On March 10, 1909, the eleventh assembly of the Montana Legislature passed a resolution favoring the establishment of Glacier National Park, but no record has been found that this resolution was ever presented to or placed in the records of either House of Congress of the United States. By an Act of February 11, 1911, the twelfth assembly of the Legislature of the State of Montana ceded exclusive jurisdiction over Glacier National Park to the United States, reserving to themselves only the right of taxation and the right to serve criminal process for acts committed outside the boundaries of the park. A few days later Senator Carter introduced a bill in the Senate of the United States to accept the cession of the park, but the bill was not reported out of committee and died there. It was not until 1914, by an act approved on August 22, that the Congress accepted from the State of Montana exclusive jurisdiction over the park, as specified by the state.

CHAPTER III

History As A National Park

THE ADMINISTRATIVE STORY

Coming of Major Logan

The first few years following the establishment of this area as a National Park saw a considerable amount of history in the making. Effective August 8, 1910, the Secretary of the Interior commissioned Major William R. Logan, who had accompanied Raphael Pumpelly through the park in 1882 and 1883, as "Superintendent of Road and Trail Construction" for the park. Previous to this time Major Logan had been Superintendent of the Indian Training School at Fort Belknap, Montana, and "Supervisor of Industries, Indian Service, at Large." On December 1, 1910, he was appointed "Inspector in Charge," of Glacier National Park, pending the establishment of the position of Superintendent, which came about on April 1, 1911.

When the Major arrived at the park, in the late summer of 1910, he brought with him his clerk, Henry W. Hutchings, who was to fill the same position in the park for many years, and also to act as interim superintendent several times. Hutchings was finally appointed to the position of Assistant Superintendent, which position he held until he retired in 1926.

The job that faced these two men that summer was anything but heartening. There were only two serviceable trails across the mountains, one from Lake McDonald across Gunsight Pass to St. Mary Lake, and the other up the McDonald Creek Valley and over Swiftcurrent Pass to Many Glacier. Old Indian trails extended across other passes but were in such a state of disuse that they were practically impassable.

To further complicate Major Logan's job, this summer was one of the worst forest fire years in the history of the northwest, and of these fires Glacier received its share. There was no organized firefighting organization as we now know it, very little equipment, few trails and practically no roads. By the time the fall rains had set in, Glacier National Park had lost over 100,000 acres of forest land to a series of fires, the largest of which covered approximately 23,000 acres.

In the fall of 1910, the first park headquarters was located at Apgar in tents. When winter came the personnel returned to Fort Belknap until spring; after making plans for establishing headquarters at Fish Creek as soon as a road could be constructed to the spot and material obtained. Also that same fall, in order to protect the area against poachers and other encroachments, Major Logan organized a patrol of six rangers, consisting of Henry Vaught

56

as Chief Ranger, Joe Cosley, Dan Doody, Bill Burns, "Dad" Randels and Pierce. For the following winter they were assigned a certain section of the park boundary to patrol.

The following summer, upon his return from Fort Belknap, Major Logan and his crew threw themselves into the task of making a National Park out of this wilderness area that had been entrusted to them. On April 1, the Major's job as Superintendent of Glacier National Park, at a salary of $3,600 per year was made permanent. For the summer he rented Apgar's cabins, at the foot of Lake McDonald, for headquarters and living quarters. The following winter he moved into the Great Northern's newly constructed Belton Chalet at the town of Belton. This move was repeated in 1912, but all the while construction was progressing on the new headquarters at Fish Creek, and in the summer of 1913 the offices were moved to this new location. The first permanent headquarters at Fish Creek consisted of six buildings, including one cottage, two cabins, and a stable, plus the old Forest Service Ranger Station that was already there, and a sawmill. The old Ranger Station was converted into an office, one cabin was used as a cookhouse, and tents were erected for the additional residences. The following winter was also spent in the Belton Chalet, but by summer of 1914 enough residences were constructed for all personnel to remain the year around.

The major accomplishments for the year 1911, in addition to the work on the new park headquarters at Fish Creek, consisted of extension of the telephone line system, rebuilding and macadamizing the road between Belton and the foot of Lake McDonald and the start of construction on the road from Apgar to Fish Creek. That summer also saw the start of construction on the predecessor to the Blackfeet Highway, from Midvale (East Glacier Park) north toward Many Glacier. This was being undertaken by the Great Northern Railway, in order to open up the northern end of the park for visitor travel. Telephone lines were constructed to Logging Ranger Station and construction started on a line to Sperry Glacier and on over Gunsight Pass to St. Mary Lake.

The Ranger Force

By 1912 a considerable amount of activity was under way in the park. Trails were being re-built, ranger cabins were constructed at various spots along the boundary for the newly organized ranger force to use, and other physical improvements were being installed and re-built. The Ranger force was expanded from the original six men to sixteen; each was assigned a portion of the park boundary to patrol constantly and ordered to look after game animals, prevent poaching, and fight forest fires. From time to time temporary rangers were employed for special jobs including that of "predatory animal hunter."

The ranger force during these early days was a rugged, hard-bitten outfit. Each foot of the park boundary was assigned to one particular man and he was responsible for the patrolling of it, winter and summer, often operating from small, crude cabins that would make the present-day patrol cabins seem like mansions. These men traveled their beat alone, and many are the tales of accidents, even deaths, resulting from these lone patrols through the mountains in the dead of winter. One ranger froze to death on the trail between cabins on the eastern side of the park; another was buried in a snowslide for twenty-four hours, yet managed to dig himself out and work his way back to the station; still another slid down a snow bank and broke his hip, which resulted in a gruelling two-day trip back to his cabin, unaided. Such were the odds against these men, yet they liked the work and would have no other. A few of the old-timers are still on the force, and others are remembered and spoken of by the local people when they get together to talk over "old times."

OLD RANGERS

The park visitor today still looks for the "Ranger" to answer his questions and help him plan his trips through the park. To him, the man in uniform is the ranger, regardless of whether he is a ranger, naturalist or park superintendent. Few people know when the term 'park ranger' came into being. It was not until 1915 that Stephen T. Mather, the Assistant Secretary of the Interior, in charge of the National Parks, wrote to all park superintendents, " . . . In order to differentiate the rangers of the national parks from those of the national forests, all rangers in the service of the national parks will be officially designated Park Rangers . . . " But to the visitor, they are still just "rangers," and probably will be for some time to come.

New Park Headquarters

Park headquarters at Fish Creek was soon inadequate for the rapidly expanding force, and plans were laid for relocating it in an area where expansion was possible. In order to accomplish this, Stephen T. Mather, then Director of the National Park Service, in 1917 purchased with his personal funds the site upon which the present headquarters and utility area now stands, from Edwin E. Snyder, who for many years conducted a hotel and saloon business at this site. The old log saloon and hotel building was then used until 1924 by the Service as a combination administration building, cookhouse, and mess hall. After that it was used as a bunkhouse for a time and torn down in 1926. In the late summer of 1917 the ground was cleared and construction was started for four residences which were completed in the summer of 1918. By the fall of 1918, a barn and wagon shed was also completed, along with a cottage for the teamster, a small warehouse, and a tower and tank for the water system, and the headquarters was moved from Fish Creek to its new location. From that time on buildings were added as necessary, building the headquarters area up to the present administrative plant.

Development of the Interpretive Services

Another interesting growth was that of the interpretive services in the park. The first so-called "Nature Guide Service" was established in 1921 as a commercial enterprise under the permit to M. P. Somes, a naturalist familiar with the park area. For a set fee, Somes conducted walking tours between hotels and chalets and other points of interest, explaining the geology, flora and fauna as he went along, much as it is done today.

In 1922 a free Nature Guide Service was established by Dr. Morton J. Elrod, of the University of Montana, under the joint sponsorship of the University and the National Park Service. To start this program, Dr. Elrod, assisted by Drs. Severy and Fredell, also of the University staff, inaugurated a series of nature walks and nature information desks in certain hotels. At first evening talks could not be held because of the lack of suitable room. This competition was hard on Somes' commercial nature guide service, and by early August he was in financial difficulties and was forced to drop his service.

Dr. Elrod continued to expand his service to the public by widening his field of operations, until, by 1927, he had one man at each of the following places: Many Glacier, Sun Camp and Lake McDonald. One gave evening talks illustrated by slides furnished by the hotel company, established self-guiding nature trails, took conducted walks and maintained cut-flower exhibits in the hotel lobbies. He also had a number of publications for sale, dealing with the natural features of the park. In 1924 he published the first Guide Book of the park, Elrod's Guide, which sold for many years as the official park guide but is now out of print and on the rare book list.

Dr. Elrod's program of nature guide   was known after 1926 as "Ranger Naturalists"—continued until 1929, when it was placed under the supervision of Dr. George C. Ruhle, the newly appointed first permanent park naturalist. The following year programs were expanded to the campgrounds with camp-fire programs; and additional nature trails were laid out, operating, as a whole, on a plan similar to that of today.

A similar development occurred in all the departments of the administration, as visitor's use of the area increased. The only lessening of activity occurred during World War II, when the park was, for all practical purposes, closed until 1946, except for the necessary maintenance and protection functions.

VISITOR USE OF THE AREA

Pre-Park Visitor Accommodations

Completion of the Great Northern Railway to this area early in 1892 brought with it the expected following of adventurers, sightseers, and settlers and marked the beginning of the settlement of the Flathead Valley and the advent of the "tourist" into what is now Glacier National Park. With these visitors and adventurers came those who saw in the land a chance for liveli-hood, in hunting, trapping, and in living off the desires of those who wished only to visit the area. These were the forerunners of the present park con-cessioners, cabin operators and dude ranchers.

Among those who arrived in 1892 and went into business were Milo Apgar and Charlie Howe, who homesteaded at the foot of Lake McDonald and put up cabins for the accommodation of visitors to the area, giving a start to the little village of Apgar, which today is one of the heavily used centers within the park boundary. In the years that followed others began to arrive both at the head and foot of Lake McDonald and they set up busi-nesses of one kind or another.

60

SNYDER HOTEL

Snyder Hotel

In 1895 George Snyder established a stopping place on Lake McDonald at the site of the present Lake McDonald Hotel. In order to take care of the increasing demand for accommodations, he was soon forced to build a hotel on the site, a two-story frame structure that was to be the focal point for visitors to the western side of the park for many years to come. In order to get the visitors to his area he had to have a boat, so he purchased a 40-foot steamboat that had been running between Somers and Polson, on Flathead Lake, and shipped it by freight to Belton. In order to bring the boat into Lake McDonald, Snyder and some other settlers had to build a road from Belton to Apgar, a rough, one-way wagon trail, but a road, nevertheless, and probably the first to exist within the boundaries of the park. When the boat arrived at Belton it was loaded with its top-heavy upright boiler, on a wagon and commenced the tortuous trip to the lake, where, after many hours of struggle, it was launched and became the first power boat to haul passengers and freight upon any of the park lakes. Mrs. Frank Liebig relates the trials of traveling up the lake on this vessel—it was too hot below deck beside the boiler and if you rode topside the sparks burned holes in your clothes.

About this same time Ed Dow, who had built a hotel at Belton a year or so earlier, started a stage line from Belton to the lake, over the newly constructed road and through the dense cedar forests that overtopped everything else in the area. It made connections with Snyder's steamboat. This was truly a beautiful trip if you were not thrown from the buckboard by the chuckholes in the road. To reach the stage, the visitors had to walk a distance of approximately one-fourth mile from the railroad station at Belton to the Middle Fork of the Flathead River, where they were ferried across in a rowboat. They were then loaded on the buckboard and started their bouncing journey to the lake and Snyder's steamboat. Such were the conditions facing the early park visitors, but they evidently enjoyed it, for many of them continued to come to the area as long as they were able to do so.

By 1896 there was a continuous chain of transportation and stopping places from the depot to the head of Lake McDonald. With Dow's hotel at Belton and his stage line to the lake, Apgar's cabins at the foot of the lake, Snyder's steamboat on the lake and his hotel and other cabins springing up at the head of the lake, the visitor was well taken care of. In addition to this, Denny Comeau and Ernest Christensen started a pack and saddle horse business at the head of Lake McDonald, taking people into the back country. In 1898 two more men, Josiah Rogers and Bert Bryant were also taking saddle horse parties out from the Lake McDonald area. At about this time Charles M. Russell, the noted cowboy artist, bought a piece of land on the shore of Lake McDonald near Apgar. Here he built his summer home, which he called "Bull Head Lodge" after the buffalo skull that was his trademark. Charlie Russell loved this area and spent a good portion of his later years at the lake painting and spinning yarns with his friends.

FIRST BRIDGE ACROSS MIDDLE FORK

First Bridge Across Middle Fork

In 1897 the first bridge was built across the Middle Fork of the Flathead, near the site of the old concrete bridge a short distance above the present park headquarters. This bridge, built by Jack Wise to enable the stages to travel the entire distance from the depot at Belton to the foot of Lake McDonald did away with the necessity of ferrying the river in rowboats.

In 1906 another boat made its appearance on Lake McDonald—a gas boat operated by Frank Kelly, which was soon joined by another, running competition to Snyder's steamboat. By 1911, when the Glacier National Park started granting concessions for commercial operations within its boundaries, there were several boats on the lake, as well as one on St. Mary Lake.

Early Park Concessioners

With the establishment of the park all concessioners for transporting and housing visitors on other than private lands came under Federal control and subject to permit. For some time permits were issued automatically to those who had been operating previously in the area, but later choice of concessioners became more selective. In 1911 permits were issued for passenger launches on St. Mary and McDonald Lakes; a stage line from Belton to Lake McDonald, run by John Weightman; saddle and pack horse permits to Josiah Rogers, W. J. Hilligoss, W. L. Adair, Cyrus Bellah, Chester Gephart, Norman Powell and Walter Gibb, and a permit for John Lewis to operate "rest cabins" near the head of Lake McDonald, including the Snyder Hotel which he had purchased in 1896

Glacier Park Hotel Company

Prior to 1910, the Great Northern Railway, anticipating the increase in passenger travel to this area resulting from the establishment of the park, had given considerable leadership to the movement for enabling legislation, and had also taken the preliminary steps toward development of the area. However, it was not until 1911 that the railway started actual development of the visitor accommodations within the park. At this time they started the construction of a number of hotels and camps, including temporary camps at the narrows of St. Mary Lake (Sun Camp) and Many Glacier, and the start of construction on the permanent buildings at Two Medicine Lake. Construction was also begun on the Glacier Park Hotel at East Glacier (Midvale) at this time, along with a series of chalets at Belton, for the accommodation of passengers disembarking from the trains at these places. A line of tent camps put up that summer by W. J. Hilligoss, for the accommodation of his saddle horse parties, were backed by the Great Northern. Their locations in Midvale (East Glacier Park), Two Medicine, Cut Bank Creek, St. Mary Lake, Gunsight Lake and near the present Sperry Chalet gave him a continuous line of camps from Midvale to Lake McDonald.

Original Lewis Hotel

During the winter of 1913-14, John Lewis built the Lewis Hotel, now Lake McDonald Hotel near the site of the original Snyder Hotel which he had previously purchased. Construction of this 65-room hotel was a colossal undertaking at that time, when it is considered that all the materials not available locally had to be hauled from the railroad at Belton to the foot of Lake McDonald

ORIGINAL LEWIS HOTEL

and then transported by boat to the hotel site, nearly 10 miles up the lake. Later Lewis removed the sixteen cabins that had been built and operated only the hotel until it was sold to the National Park Service in 1930, but continued under operation of the Great Northern.

Work was going full-speed on the Great Northern buildings in various areas of the park. By 1913 the following accommodations were completed and in use or ready for use: the main hotel building, one chalet, two dormitories and several utility buildings at Glacier Park Station, the larger chalet at Two Medicine, Cut Bank and St. Mary Chalets, a dining room and eight chalets at Sun Camp, Sperry Chalets, and a tent camp with a dining room and dormitory at Gunsight Lake.

When we stop and think a moment about the scope and hardships involved in this building activity we can but marvel at the ingenuity shown by these

GOING-TO-THE-SUN CHALETS

construction crews. At many Glacier a sawmill was built to cut building material from the surrounding forest. The large timbers in the lobbies of Glacier Park and Many Glacier Hotels were hauled and skidded for several miles to the hotel site. Native stone was quarried for foundations and fireplaces. And a tremendous quantity of supplies and building materials hauled by team and wagon over primitive dirt roads from the rail head at Glacier Park Station, including the large boilers and other massive equipment that went into the construction of what was at one time the largest hotel in the state.

Many Glacier Hotel

The immense posts in the Glacier Park Lodge were hauled in by trainloads from western Washington and erected on the site by what would now be considered primitive means. What would you and I have done if faced with the problem of building the large stone buildings at Sperry Chalet, high in the mountains and reached only by boat and trail? I am content merely to ponder. But we must recognize the difficulties involved and the large amount of money spent by this company to develop these large, luxurious stopping places in the heart of the wilderness.

To Louis W. Hill, then president of the Great Northern Railway, goes the credit for this initial development of the park and establishment of these first large concessions. Hill was always an enthusiastic admirer of the park, both

65

because of its economic value to the railroad and because of his personal love of the park. He devoted much of his time to the planning and organizing of this development, and practically every department of the Great Northern was

MANY GLACIER HOTEL

called upon at one time or another to make their contribution to the development of this wilderness area for visitor use.

By 1915 Granite Park Chalets and the Many Glacier Hotel were completed and opened for business; this completed and put into operation the major portion of the Great Northern Hotels in the park. These, along with the private hotels and cabins on Lake McDonald, could now furnish sumptuous quarters and living for as many visitors as the railroad could bring into the area. In 1917 the newly-formed "Glacier Park Hotel Company," charged with operating these hotels and chalets, signed its first twenty-year operation contract with the Department of the Interior.

Prince of Wales Hotel

In 1926 the Glacier Park Hotel Company started construction of a Swiss-type hotel in Waterton Lakes National Park, just north of the Canadian boundary in Alberta. This beautiful hotel on a hill overlooking Waterton Lakes, which was opened for business on July 25, 1927, completed the chain of Great Northern Hotels and Chalets in the area. Further contracts were negotiated with the company from time to time, and the company is still operating these

PRINCE OF WALES HOTEL

units as they did years ago, with the exception of Cut Bank, St. Mary, and Going-to-the-Sun Chalets, which were closed down during or prior to World War II and never re-opened. All three of these Chalets were razed in recent years because of their physical condition, lack of business, and lack of money to repair them and keep them in operation. In 1933 the company opened their first cabin camp at Swiftcurrent, near the Many Glacier Hotel, most of which was destroyed by the 1936 forest fire and rebuilt again in 1937. In 1941 a coffee shop was added at Swiftcurrent and the cabin camp and coffee shop at East Glacier (Rising Sun) was opened for business. In 1961 operations of the concessions hotel and motel buildings, camp stores and dining rooms, the transportation company and the launch International were assumed by Glacier Park Incorporated, a new company which purchased the interests of the Glacier Park Company and was awarded a 20-year concessions contract by the National Park Service.

Lake McDonald Hotel

In February of 1930 a series of negotiations took place in which the Dakota and Great Northern Township Company, a subsidiary of the Great Northern, took up their option to purchase the Lewis Hotel on Lake McDonald. This

LAKE McDONALD HOTEL

company thus gained possession of the hotel and utility buildings, along with 285 acres of land on the lake shore, with the intent to hold it, clear the title, and turn it over to the Federal Government. Consequently, in 1932, the National Park Service purchased this property for over $150,000 and then leased it to the Glacier Park Hotel Company, an arrangement that is still in effect.

The Glacier Park Hotel Company, although the largest single hotel operator in the area, was by no means the only one in the park. As the years went by, more and more private operators were putting up cabins and small hotels in or near the park. Cabin camps and hotels arose in the small town adjacent to the area and other camps sprang up on private lands within the park, mainly around Lake McDonald. But as these accommodations increased, so did the travel, and even today, with new modern camps and motels being erected throughout the area, there is still a shortage of places in which to stay.

Skyland Camps

One of the unusual camps to operate within the park was the Skyland Camp, with headquarters on Bowman Lake. It opened for business in 1922, serving mainly as a boys' camp from July 2 to August 27 and as a tourist camp for the remainder of the time between June 15 and snowfall. The camp was operated by the Culver Military Academy of Culver, Indiana, and catered to teenage boys who could take care of themselves in the woods with the proper leadership and guidance. The main camp at Bowman Lake consisted of a log lodge and dining room, several outbuildings and tent sleeping quarters. The subsidiary camps at Upper and Lower Kintla Lakes were all of canvas construction with the exception of a log dining room at Lower Kintla Lake. The tourist camp at Bowman which was open all summer, consisted of a four-room chalet and tents. Hiking and saddle trips were taken from these camps throughout the park, connecting them with the other operators' accommodations in the area. This camp operated for several years, but finally closed down because of lack of business.

The Bell Ringers

During the latter part of August 1925, W. R. Mills, then advertising agent of the Great Northern Railway, and H. A. Noble, manager of the Glacier Park Hotel Company, made a request of the park superintendent for permission to place locomotive bells on the summits of the following passes in the park: Swiftcurrent, Logan, Siyeh, Gunsight, Cut Bank, Stoney Indian and at Grinnell Glacier. This request was based upon an old Swiss custom of having bells on the mountain tops and passes and the desire to give the visitors hiking or riding through the park the unusual experience of ringing these loud, clear bells high in the mountains.

PIEGAN PASS BELL

The request was passed on to the office of the Director of the National Park Service, who did not approve of the idea but was somewhat loath to say so at the time, so the decision was postponed. Mr. Noble continued to press for the bells, and finally in September of 1926 the request was granted for at least two bells to be established in these passes. Within the next two months the company had placed three of them on Swiftcurrent, Piegan and Siyeh passes. These bells were bought by the Hotel Company at a cost of $194.27 each, plus packing, shipping and the expense of placing them. They were very beautifully toned and created a considerable amount of interest among the people who crossed these passes and heard them ring.

A fourth bell was placed on Mt. Henry, where the Glacier Park-Two Medicine Trail crosses Scenic Point, high above Lower Two Medicine Lake, in the summer of 1929. These four bells remained in place until the fall of 1943, when they were removed by the Hotel Company and turned in on a World War II scrap metal drive.

Saddle Horse Operators

Near the turn of the century Comeau, Christensen, Bryant and Rogers started taking visitors out into the park on saddle horse trips, and Snyder's steamboat started operating on Lake McDonald. At this time the pattern was set for visitor use of trails in the park area, and the region began to build up the saddle horse business that was later to give Glacier the name of a trail park.

The small operators continued to expand their services, operating mostly from their home camps but using pack strings to extend their trips over longer periods of time. It was not until 1911, after the park was established, that the first semi-permanent type of tent camps came into being, thereby enabling saddle horse parties to travel long distances through the park without having to set up camp each night. In this year, W. J. Hilligoss, backed by the Great Northern Railway, set up a string of tent camps between the main disembarking point at Midvale, (East Glacier) and the Lake McDonald Hotel, for the accommodation of saddle horse parties. Also, within the next few years, the Glacier Park Hotel Company's chalets and hotels came into being, affording additional stop-overs for the saddle and hiking parties.

Until 1915 the saddle horse business within the park consisted of a number of independent operators, each under permit to the National Park Service and each operating in his own manner and at his own price. In 1915, under the leadership of W. N. Noffsinger, an attorney from Kalispell, Montana, a number of these small concessioners were combined as the Park Saddle Horse Company with their base ranch on the St. Mary River, several miles east of the park near Babb, Montana. This company then obtained a concession contract with the National Park Service and became the official saddle horse operator in the area.

The Park Saddle Horse Company continued to expand under the brand —X6 (Bar X Six) until at one time it owned over 1,000 head of horses and was the largest saddle horse outfit of its kind in the world, handling over 10,000 park visitors a year on the park trails. The advent of the automobile and the Going-to-the-Sun Road cut into this method of travel severely, and at the time the company ceased operations in 1942, they were not handling over 5,000 persons per year.

In 1924 when W. N. Noffsinger died, his son George W. Noffsinger took over and continued the business. The following summer he initiated what was known as the North Circle Trip, a five-day tour, with stops at tent camps or chalets, such as Hilligoss had established in 1911. Three permanent tent

70

SADDLE PARTY

camps were placed in operation at Fifty Mountain, Goathaunt (at the head of Waterton Lake), and at Crossley Lake on the Belly River. These camps coupled with Granite Park Chalets constituted a tour made up of five one-day rides, starting and ending at Many Glacier Hotel. Another camp was established at Red Eagle Lake in 1926 which, along with Going-to-the-Sun, Cut Bank and Two Medicine Chalets, furnished another camp-to-camp trip from Glacier Park Station (East Glacier) to Many Glacier, known as the "Inside Trail." A third operated from Many Glacier to Sun Camp, to Sperry Chalets, Lake McDonald Hotel, Granite Park, and back to Many Glacier. These tours were very popular with both the saddle horse parties and the hikers, and were continued through 1942, after which all concessions closed down their operations because of World War II. On February 15, 1943 when Mr. Noffsinger, president of the company, formally requested the National Park Service and the Department of the Interior to terminate his contract because of financial reverses, the Park Saddle Horse Company ended its noted and somewhat unique career.

In 1946 and 1947 Mrs. Bernice Lewis of Browning, Montana operated the saddle horses in the park, and in 1948 she divided her territory with Roy W. Wessels of River Bend Ranch, West Glacier, Montana. Wessels took over the operation at Lake McDonald, leaving only the Many Glacier operation to Mrs. Lewis. In the meantime Bryant Graves had been operating from Glacier Park Station (East Glacier). Mrs. Lewis operated through 1950, when E. G. Well-

71

man, owner and operator of the Bear Creek Ranch near Essex, Montana, took over the saddle horse concessions in Glacier. In 1959 George Moore of Pablo, Montana took over the reins of the saddle horse concession and added a new operation at St. Mary.

Motor Transportation

The third type of visitor service in the park was motor transportation which, though slower to get under way than the saddle horses, nevertheless played a great part in increasing the use of the area. Although motorized public transportation did not make its appearance until 1914, prior to this there were a few horsedrawn stage lines to take park visitors from place to place. The first such venture of which we have record was Ed Dow's buckboard stage from Belton to the foot of Lake McDonald. Later John Weightman put in on the same run, a line of "fringe-topped" surreys which transported passengers from the trains to the lake.

In 1911 the first automobile appeared in Glacier National Park. The vehicle was owned by Frank Stoop, a garage man from Kalispell, founder of the present Stoop's Garage, and it was driven by Frank Whalen, one of Stoop's mechanics and later chief mechanic for the park. The party made their way to the end of the dirt road at Lake Five, about five miles from Belton, then followed the railroad tracks for the remainder of the journey.

The first automobile to be driven over the newly opened road into Many Glacier was one carrying Louis W. Hill and party, of the Great Northern Railway, on August 7, 1914. This car was driven by Fred A. Noble, retired general manager of the Glacier Park Transportation Company. On August 17, just ten days later, a $1.00 entrance fee was collected from the auto of Levi Bird, quite probably the first auto fee collected in the park and certainly the first one in Many Glacier Valley.

In the year 1912 the first transportation company was started on the eastern side of the park by the Brewster Brothers, headed by W. A. Brewster. This concession consisted of three horse-drawn stage coaches drawn by four horses each and operated between the rail head at Midvale (East Glacier) and the camps of Two Medicine, Cut Bank, St. Mary and Many Glacier. They made the trip to Many Glacier in two days with an overnight stop at St. Mary.

The Brewsters, though, were soon destined to bow before modern transportation methods. In the spring of 1914 a rival company appeared on the scene, the newly organized "Glacier Park Transportation Company," owned by Rowe Emery and backed by the White Motor Company. On April 24, 1914, this new company made application for and received permission to operate the sole passenger and freight concession within Glacier National Park. On June 5, 1914 they entered into their first official contract with the Department of the Interior, and the business was under way.

Mr. Emery hired A. K. Holmes as manager of the company, imported ten buses, five touring cars, and a couple of trucks, all from the White Motor Company, and started operation in earnest, very effectively eliminating the Brewster Brothers from the transportation picture. These buses, primitive by present day standards, had stationary wooden tops supported by iron brackets and side curtains to keep out the rain and wind whenever necessary. Along the length of the buses on either side was a large wooden sign mounted on brackets—"Glacier Park Transportation Company." These signs broke off on almost every trip and had to be replaced, so they were finally removed.

The early days of this company were days of trials and tribulations. The first year, 1914, was relatively dry, but much of the new road up the eastern front of the range had to be repaired and in places the dips filled in to keep from tearing off the baggage racks on the rear of the long buses. But the venture was quite successful and business looked good. Then in 1915 came one of those seasons in which it rained almost every day. The roads became a sea of mud, and the buses had to be pulled across certain sections of the road with horses. Often they spent as much time off the road as on it, and the passengers arrived at their destination muddy, scared, tired and wish-

OLD BUSES

ing they were back home. It is to the credit of Mr. Holmes and his drivers that this operation was able to continue through the summer; although at times ready to give up, Emery was willing to give it one more try and in the end managed to make it through the season. With this experience behind them, the company was ready for anything, continued to enlarge and soon covered the entire park.

In the year 1927 Emery sold out to a new company, the Glacier Transport Company, owned by Mr. Howard H. Hays and associates. Mr. Hays, now a newspaper publisher in Riverside, California, had previously had transport experience in Yellowstone National Park, and also owned and operated the transportation company in Sequoia and Kings Canyon National Parks. This company continued to improve and enlarge and by 1930 was operating a fleet of over 65 buses in the park. At the present time Glacier Park Incorporated has the sole motor transportation concession in the park, and their fleet of large, red sight-seeing buses carry thousands of visitors over the park

73

roads every summer, continuing the traditions of safety and courtesy established by the owners and drivers in the early days when the going was at its worst. The Transport Company was sold by Hays and associates to the Glacier Park Company in 1957 (who sold it in turn to Glacier Park Incorporated in 1961.)

Boat Operators

The third method of commercial transportation in the park is by boat, which has afforded many hours of pleasure to the park visitors, as well as a useful means of transportation from one spot to another. Here, again, the first known boat transportation occurred on Lake McDonald, with the advent of Snyder's steamboat, the F. I. Whitney in 1895, followed by Frank Kelly's boats in 1906. The fleet of boats on Lake McDonald had increased to five by 1910.

In 1911, the first year in which the park granted permits or concessions to operators, Messrs Denny and Kelly were given permits to operate three boats on Lake McDonald, carrying one hundred twenty-five, twenty-five, and

LAUNCH ST. MARY
—HAYNES PICTURE SHOPS INC.

twenty-five persons respectively. At the same time one James T. Maher was given a permit to operate a forty-foot, twenty-passenger launch on St. Mary Lake, running from St. Mary to the camp at the site of the Going-to-the-Sun Chalets, near the upper end of the lake. The following year the Great Northern was given a permit to operate two boats on St. Mary Lake, to supply and transport passengers to "Sun Camp." The "Red Eagle" and the "Glacier," each gas operated, thirty-two feet long and with a capacity of twenty-five persons each, started operation in June, 1912. In 1913 the "Red Eagle" was replaced by the "St. Mary," a gas powered boat sixty-four feet long with a fourteen foot beam, capable of carrying seventy-five passengers from St. Mary to Sun Camp. This boat operated on St. Mary Lake until the opening of the Going-to-the-Sun Road, when it was retired from use. In 1951 it was sold to Bernard Rankin, then Superintendent of State Parks of Montana, and is now again in use hauling passengers on Flathead Lake.

In 1914, a colorful character appeared on the boat scene in the park. When Captain "Billy" Swanson, a boat builder and operator on Flathead Lake, decided that the pastures were a little greener in the park, he decided to take his boat, the sixty-foot "City of Polson" up to Lake McDonald via the water route. After many trials and tribulations, the lesser of which included much hauling by shore lines, the boat finally reached the lake, having come all the way up the Flathead River and McDonald Creek by water. After reaching the lake, he added eleven feet to the boat's length, renamed it the "Lewtana" and used it with the Kelly and Denny fleet. After Denny left, Swanson went into business with Kelly and Snyder on the Lake.

Of all the park concessions, the boat operators present the most confusing picture, particularly during the 1920's, with different companies, including the hotel company, operating on different lakes, and many of the operations were to change hands.

In 1920 Captain Swanson, who had heretofore been operating with Kelly and Snyder on Lake McDonald, built a forty-passenger launch on Two Medicine Lake and put it into operation for the Hotel Company. By this time the Hotel Company was in the boat business on Two Medicine, St. Mary and Mc Dermott (Swiftcurrent) Lakes, the latter only to the extent of renting row boats. Kelly continued his operation on Lake McDonald.

In 1921 the boat concession on Lake McDonald was taken over from Frank Kelly by R. C. Abell, and consisted of three passenger boats, with Captain Swanson again back on the lake in charge of them. Abell only operated for three years, though, when he sold to the Glacier Park Transport Company, and Captain Anderson of Flathead Lake became manager of these boats. Swanson then obtained the boat concession on the east side of the park, with the exception of the St. Mary, and started building launches for McDermott Lake at Many Glacier.

75

LAUNCH INTERNATIONAL, WATERTON LAKE

In 1927 and 1928, Captain Swanson built, for the Glacier Park Hotel Company, the launch "International" which was put into service on Waterton Lake in the summer of 1928. This boat, seventy-three feet long with a sixteen foot beam, carried two engines operating twin screws, and was capable of carrying two hundred and fifty passengers. This largest of the park launches is still operating on Waterton Lake from the town of Waterton, in Alberta, to the southern end of the lake, in Glacier National Park.

In 1938 Swanson sold his interest in the Swanson Boat Company to Arthur J. Burch, of Kalispell, and Captain Anderson. The operation then became known as the Glacier Park Boat Company; then as today, it operated the boats on Two Medicine and Swiftcurrent Lakes. In 1946 the interests of Mrs. Melanie Anderson, Captain Anderson's widow, were assigned to Arthur Burch, leaving him sole owner of the Company. By this time there were three major boat operators in the park: The Glacier Park Boat Company; The Glacier Park Hotel Company, operating the Launch International on Waterton Lake;

LAUNCH "RED EAGLE" ON ST. MARY LAKE
H. H. NEWS PHOTO

and The Glacier Park Transport Company, operating the row boats and the Launch "DeSmet," on Lake McDonald. In the summer of 1953 the Glacier Park Transport Company sold their interests on Lake McDonald to Arthur M. Burch (son of the owner of the Glacier Park Boat Company) and Raymond L. Simpson.

This new operation on Lake McDonald became the Lake McDonald Boat Company, operating only on this lake until 1957 when they expanded to include St. Mary Lake. In 1956 Stan-Craft built in Kalispell, Montana, the hull for a new excursion launch, which was thirty-eight feet in length with a ten foot beam. Burch and Simpson completed the interior and superstructure to accommodate forty passengers. The new launch "Red Eagle" is powered by two gas-driven engines with twin screws. In October, 1958 Arthur Burch assumed the interests of Ray Simpson and became the sole owner and operator of the Lake McDonald Boat Company.

Park Visitation

It is hard to say just when this area first assumed its role as a major recreational attraction. Many of the early explorers may have considered their journeys into these mountains as a recreational activity, while to others it probably was a lot of hard work. But we do know that with the coming of the Great Northern Railway the area, particularly around Lake McDonald, became a major attraction to people from the east, encouraged no doubt by the tales and writings of such people as Dr. Lyman B. Sperry, George Bird Grinnell, and James Willard Schultz.

We have no way of knowing how many people entered the area prior to 1911, for no methods of counting them were in existence and no one was particularly interested in doing so. But by 1900 the business of catering to the wants of these visitors was a big business and has continued to increase in size, year by year, ever since.

Name Changes

Such a growth in use of an area not only brings with it wealth and benefits to those who supply the needs of visitors, but it also brings its "growing pains," and its unusual or unexpected turn of events. One of these unexpected turns resulted from such a simple matter as changing the name of a town.

In 1934 and 1935 the residents of the town of Belton, at the western entrance to the park, wishing to identify themselves more closely with the park, made a concerted effort to have the name "Belton" changed to "West Glacier." This was backed by the National Park Service and had the support of the president of the Great Northern Railway. A petition was drawn up and signed by the residents, but for some reason there was a lack of followup action and the movement died. At the same time there was some discussion relative to changing the name of Glacier Park Station, formerly Midvale, to East Glacier, for similar reasons. This change was discouraged by the park superintendent and nothing further was done on it.

Again in 1949, this time headed by the Columbia Falls newspaper "Hungry Horse News," and the West Glacier Lions Club, the change was again brought up and carried through, changing the name of Belton to "West Glacier," effective October 1, 1949. But this time the Great Northern did not go along with the idea, and the town ended up with two names; the post office and that portion north of the railroad tracks becoming West Glacier, and the railroad depot and that portion of the old townsite south of the tracks remaining as Belton. From here on things began to get complicated.

The following year, Glacier Park Station, wishing to create a corresponding name on the east side of the park, changed its name to "East Glacier Park," which shortened locally to become "East Glacier." Here again, the railroad refused to concur and retained the name of Glacier Park Station for their station. This immediately caused confusion in the park, for the cabin camp and campground at Roes Creek, on St. Mary Lake, had been officially called East Glacier, so that name came up for revision. When park officials, at Ed Beatty's suggestion, finally settled on the name "Rising Sun" for the development at Roes Creek, things settled down to an even keel again, except in the minds of those who resided in or who had visited the area previously. To them the change will not be reconciled for many years, but in time all will again be serene.

Famous Visitors to the Area

Any area open to public use, particularly one of national significance, is sooner or later visited by one or more people of some degree of national or international fame. Of these, Glacier has had several whose claim to fame has had world-wide recognition. One of the first of these internationally known figures was Lincoln Ellsworth, who later was the guiding financial genius for the Amundsen polar expedition of 1926. Ellsworth first visited the park in 1911; for about a month he traveled over the area accompanied by Ranger James C. Graves. He returned in 1912, and again in the summer of 1926, when Captain Roald Amundsen, the famed North Pole flier, and his crew from the dirigible "Norge," stopped briefly at Glacier Park Station, on their way from Alaska, following their successful flight over the north pole. The flight from Nome, over the north pole and down to Alaska was one of the famous polar flights, and the first successful one over the pole. With the captain and his crew was Lincoln Ellsworth.

Also in the year 1926, on November 8, Queen Marie of Rumania stopped briefly at Glacier Park Station on her way west and was welcomed by a large aggregation of Blackfeet Indians. Their ceremony was conducted entirely by

PRESIDENT FRANKLIN D. ROOSEVELT

the Indians, the only white persons participating in any way being the members of the Queen's own party. In a circle of Indian tepees on the lawn of the Glacier Park Hotel, with the snow-capped mountains of the park as a backdrop, the Queen, Princess Ileana, and Prince Nicholas were adopted into the Blackfeet tribe, given appropriate Indian names, and were presented with buckskin garments and war bonnets. Following the ceremony, Superintendent and Mrs. Kraebel were presented to the Queen and her party.

The next notable visit was that of President Franklin D. Roosevelt on August 5, 1934. On the morning of August 5, the President and his official party entered the park at Belton, well escorted by police, park rangers and secret service men, were taken over the Going-to-the-Sun Road to St. Mary. From there the party went south to the Two Medicine Chalets where the President, Mrs. Roosevelt, and Secretary of the Interior Harold L. Ickes were inducted into the Blackfeet Indian tribe. Following this the President made one of his famous fireside radio broadcasts from the chalet, and was then taken to Glacier Park Station where he boarded his special train for Washington, D. C. This was the first time that a president of the United States had visited

SECRETARY ICKES

81

Glacier National Park. While on his trip through the park, the Blackfeet Indians also gave the President a peace pipe, supposedly the one that had been used to seal the treaty of 1855 between the United States and the Blackfeet Nation at Judith Basin, Montana.

CROWN PRINCE OLAF AND PRINCESS MARTHA OF NORWAY

In 1939 royalty again visited Glacier National Park, when Crown Prince Olav and Princess Martha of Norway visited the park from June 3 through June 5. This same year Associate Justice — later Chief Justice — Harlan Stone and his wife spent a two-week vacation in the park and were inducted into the Blackfeet tribe, as were many other notables. While in the park, Mrs. Stone did many paintings, several of which were exhibited in New York.

Although not actually a park visitor, the second president to pass by the area was Harry S. Truman who, on the evening of September 30, 1952, stopped briefly at West Glacier and talked to the people of the community. Mr. Truman was accompanied by his daughter Margaret, and several other notables. He was making the last official trip of his term of office, campaigning for his unsuccessful candidate for president, Governor Stevenson of Illinois. Over two-hundred people, along with the Columbia Falls High School Band, were present to hear him speak.

NOTABLE FOREST FIRES

Nothing has a more devastating effect than a forest fire upon a forested area and also upon the minds of the people concerned with protecting such an area. Throughout the history of mankind, fire, when controlled, has been his benefactor, when uncontrolled, it has been his greatest scourge. Forested areas throughout the world contain records, written and unwritten, of forest fires that swept over vast areas leaving nothing behind but blackened ruins which Nature patiently set about to restore. Such is the story of the forested areas in Glacier National Park; contained within the written records are the stories of a number of disastrous fires and fire-years that even yet cause men to shudder when they look back upon them.

One of the worst fire-years in the history of the Pacific Northwest was 1910 when hundreds of thousands of acres of forest were burning at the same time. Extremely dry weather, high winds, and lightning storms had made torches out of thousands of square miles of virgin forest in Washington, northern Idaho, and western Montana. And of the fires, Glacier National Park received its share. Although the park had just been created and Major Logan had been sent in from the Indian Service to set up an organization to administer it, practically all his time until the fall rains came was diverted into attempting to control these devastating fires. There was no firefighting organization then, as we know it now, little equipment, few trails and no roads. Everything had to be done the hard way, and there were too few people to do it. With fires cropping up all over the western slopes of the mountain ranges, it is no wonder that over 100,000 acres of the park burned over.

The major conflagration, caused mainly by dry-lightning storms, consisted of 23,000 acres below Kintla Creek, extending from Ford Creek to the Canadian boundary and from the Flathead River to the mountains. Because of a careless camper another 8,000 acres burned around the foot of Bowman Lake; this area extended from a point about two miles down the creek from the lake, up both shores to the foot of the mountains. "Spot fires" from fires across the North Fork, on the Whitefish Range, accounted for another 19,000 acres including almost all of the lower reaches of Camas, Dutch and Anaconda Creeks. 7,600 acres burned over above Nyack, across the river from Garry Lookout, and 4,000 acres went up in smoke at Red Eagle, from unknown causes, as well as dozens of others of a lesser extent throughout the western slopes of the park. This same siege of fires saw the Upper Ole Creek drainage,

Fielding and the southeastern corner of the park as far as Midvale (East Glacier Park) also burned over.

As is usually the case, bad fire-years occur only periodically, with little or no set pattern. It was not until 1920 that the park was again beset with conditions of weather that caused any extensive forest fires. In that year there were three badly burned areas, including between 1,500 and 2,000 acres on Dutch Creek, 150 to 200 acres on Lincoln Creek and 200 to 300 acres on Huckleberry Mountain. By this time the park had a much better firefighting organization than in earlier days and undoubtedly much better control over those fires that did get started.

The year 1926 saw the next bad fire-year, reportedly the worst since 1910. Fires began in the park in May and continued until mid-August. Director Albright came out to the park and personally took charge of the fire situation during the month of August. Over seven hundred men were employed in twenty-five fire camps at one time. During this time twenty-three fires burned over a total of 50,000 acres, the worst being one that burned the forested Apgar Mountain-Lake McDonald area. Although another 300-acre blaze near Lake McDermott (Swiftcurrent) threatened to be equally as serious, but it was finally controlled.

The year 1929 was dry and potentially dangerous for fire, but the park had been relatively lucky, with no fires of any consequence. Then, on August 16, a slash fire, burning on private logging operations between eight and ten miles outside the park boundary, near Columbia Falls, escaped from its bounds under high winds and low humidity conditions, and the famous Halfmoon Fire of 1929 was underway. It overran the logging crews of the Halfmoon Lumber Company and forest crews were sent to stop the fire. Carrying as a crown fire across portions of the Flathead and Blackfeet National Forests, on August 21 it jumped the North Fork of the Flathead River into the park, near its southwestern corner. From there the fire spread rapidly eastward, on both sides of the Middle Fork of the Flathead River toward Belton and Lake McDonald. By some miracle of fate, it missed Park Headquarters, Belton and most of Apgar, but continued eastward almost to Nyack before being stopped.

All fire control agencies in the northwest were called in on this fire and personnel came from all over the United States. Fire Control Expert John Coffman, of the National Park Service, arrived on the 22nd and personally took charge of the park organization, but before it was over the park lost over 50,000 acres of fine forest, of which about 10,000 acres was a heavy stand of reproduction from previous burns. The entire fire burned, both inside and outside the park, approximately 103,000 acres at a total cost of over $300,000., $244,000 of which was expended by Glacier National Park. Those who drive along the road between West Glacier and the foot of Lake McDonald today do not see the devastation wrought by this fire, as the old burn is being rapidly replaced by a thriving crop of lodgepole pine, replacing the majestic stand of redcedars and hemlock that were there prior to 1929.

1935 saw two other devastating fires, at the same time at opposite ends of the park. The first, the Kennedy Creek Fire, started on August 6 by a spark from a campfire on Kennedy Creek (Otatso Creek), several miles inside the park boundary. Under a high wind it spread rapidly to the east burning out the lower reaches of the Kennedy Creek Valley, including the Kennedy Creek Ranger Station buildings and spread out onto the Blackfeet Indian Reservation. 555 acres were burned in the park and 2,654 acres on Indian lands.

The day following the start of the Kennedy Creek Fire, a lightning strike started another fire on Boundary Creek, almost on the Canadian Line, west of Waterton Lake. Crews reached the fire and had it under control until, on August 9, high winds took it over the control lines and on its way toward Waterton Lake and the town of Waterton in Alberta. When finally stopped by the cooperative effort of both Glacier and Waterton crews, it was within one and one-half miles of the town and had burned 988 acres in Glacier and 1,244 acres in Waterton National Park, including the timber on about two and a half miles of the shore line of Waterton Lake.

One of the most disastrous fires in the history of the park, with the possible exception of the Halfmoon Fire of 1929, was the Heavens Peak Fire of August 1936. On August 19 lightning struck a tree on the southeastern shoulder of Heavens Peak, known as the Glacier Wall, and started a small fire. When the smoke was discovered on August 21, men were sent out to suppress the fire, but the precipitous nature of the terrain made it very difficult to control; it had reached an area of approximately 200 acres before the spread was stopped. Everything was going fine, and the fire was thought to be under control, when, on August 31, high winds came up and the fire flared up, jumped the control lines and started for Granite Park and Swiftcurrent Pass. The following day it reached Granite Park and that evening, by 8:00 o'clock, crossed Swiftcurrent Pass and was roaring down the Many Glacier Valley, a rolling wall of flame. Within a matter of hours it reached and passed the Many Glacier Hotel, which it spared; but it burned out most of the Swiftcurrent cabins, the government ranger station, the museum and other buildings on Swiftcurrent Lake. A change in the wind and weather stopped the blaze before it had a chance to go much farther, and fire fighting crews were then able to move in and take steps to prevent its further spread and damage. This fire burned approximately 7,500 acres and, from the standpoint of the park visitor, was the most devastating fire in the park, as it completely denuded one of the most beautiful valleys in the park and partially stripped another, both of which were on main traveled routes or visitor concentration areas.

The next bad fire-year occurred in 1940, when dry lightning storms

85

set over twenty fires, several of which reached pro'ect proportions. The largest on Nyack Creek, burned over 420 acres, while the next largest, above Bowman Lake, burned approximately 300 acres. Many other smaller blazes at the same time taxed the firefighting strength of the park and required outside aid from those agencies who could spare men from their own fires.

It was not until 1945 that another bad fire burned within the park boundaries. In this year the Curly Bear Fire burned over 280 acres just below the lookout station on Curly Bear Mountain. This lightning-caused fire cost the park $14,636 to suppress.

More than a decade passed before the next major fire occurred in the park. 1958 was the last of the bad fire-years when approximately 3,000 acres burned over in thirty-three fires, of which twenty-six were caused by lightning, the remainder by man. The largest of the fires was the Coal Creek Fire which burned 2,534 acres. This was a man-caused fire that cost the park $219,801 for manpower, equipment and other expenditures. The use of borate solution, sprayed by airplanes, kept this blaze from being more disastrous than it was.

Most of the fires in 1958 occurred during the month of August when the area was continually besieged with dry lightning storms. With many fires burning at one time, the manpower was spread very thin over the park fighting fires from a negligible size up to the Razoredge Mountain Fire of 153 acres in addition to the Coal Creek Fire. The total expenditure for fire suppression during the year was $254,846.13.

The above-mentioned fires were not the only bad ones, but represent the worst fire conditions through the years. Such conditions will undoubtedly arise again and again, but with increased knowledge and better fire equipment man is slowly making headway in his battle to control and prevent the recurrence of such catastrophies as occurred in 1929, 1936 and 1958.

ROADS AND TRAILS

Early Road Builders

The earliest roads in Glacier National Park were built just prior to the turn of the century, during the late 1890's. At this point, we are using the term "road" quite loosely, for those early roads were little more than "routes" over which it was possible to take a team and wagon to haul supplies from the railroad to a nearby settlement. Most of them grew out of necessity rather than planning, and followed the paths of least resistance.

One of the earliest was the route, cleared between the village of Belton and the foot of Lake McDonald, over which Snyder hauled his steamboat in 1895, and over which Dow's buckboards bounced and plunged hauling visitors from the railroad depot to Apgar on their way to the head of the lake. Oldtimers speak of the dense forest of large redcedar trees that covered the Apgar Flats through which this road wound, taking one's mind off the condition of the trip with their primitive beauty.

In 1901, with the start of oil drilling activity at Kintla Lake, the Butte Oil Company extended this road some forty miles to the foot of Kintla Lake, over the same general route as the present North Fork Road. Here, again, one must stretch his imagination to picture it as a road, according to present day standards. No grading was done, and no bridges were built. Corduroy (short pieces of log laid crosswise) was placed across the worst mud holes, and the necessary trees were cut to allow the wagons to pass. That was the first North Fork Road. But in spite of this, the road was built, and most of the heavy machinery for the well at Kintla Lake was hauled over it during the first summer.

This road was little improved over the next ten years, until the establishment of the park in 1910. One of Major Logan's first jobs as superintendent of the park was to rebuild and macadamize or hard surface the road between Belton and Lake McDonald, and start construction of a continuation around the lake toward the proposed headquarters area at the mouth of Fish Creek. The Belton-Apgar section was completed in 1912 and the Fish Creek Road in 1913, giving for the first time a good roadway from the railroad to the lake. In 1915 work was started on the rebuilding of the North Fork Road, and by the end of the summer it was practically completed to the top of McGee Hill. This road was soon completed to Logging Creek and later to Polebridge, opening up the North Fork of the Flathead to much easier methods of travel.

Almost coincident with the start of the Belton-Apgar Road was the establishment of a freight road from Fort Browning into the Many Glacier Valley, to supply the mining camps and new boom town of Altyn. Here, again, necessity was the motivating factor, and the road followed the path of least resistance, but in this case the open prairie-like country afforded much easier access, except during wet weather. Evidences of many of these olden-day freight roads may still be found, usually consisting only of a few weed-choked ruts through the brush thickets—mute evidence of the transportation difficulties of those times.

In 1911, when the Great Northern Railway started to build its hotels and chalets along the eastern side of the park, they immediately ran into transportation difficulties. Tons of lumber and other building materials, boilers for heating plants, supplies and equipment of all kinds had to be hauled into these mountain valleys for the construction of these large hotels. And following the construction of accommodations, the visitors had to be transported to them.

Because the administration of the park was being carried on with a minimum of funds, which did not permit any extensive road construction, the Great Northern stepped into the breach and went ahead at their own expense to construct the roads and trails needed for the necessary visitor transportation at that time. In 1911 they contracted for the first construction on a road from Midvale (East Glacier Park) to Many Glacier, the predecessor of the present Blackfeet Highway, under an agreement with the Department of the Interior. Work on this road was pushed along and in 1913, on August 7, the first automobile was driven over it to McDermott Lake; it carried the president of the Great Northern Railway, Louis W. Hill, and his party. This road opened up the route to Many Glacier, following the new construction to St. Mary, and from there the old freight road into Many Glacier, which had been improved enough to allow for heavier traffic.

The following year rebuilding was carried on toward Many Glacier, with the United States Reclamation Service completing the section between Babb and the site of their dam on Sherburne Lake, at the park boundary. The Department of the Interior completed reconstruction of the St. Mary-Babb section in 1915 and carried on to complete the final section to Many Glacier within the next few years.

This road from Midvale to Many Glacier was unsurfaced but well graded, and in dry weather was very easy to negotiate. But after a period of heavy rains this prairie mud would be nearly impossible to cross. Mr. A. K. Holmes, then general manager of the newly formed Glacier Park Transportation Company, writes that since their first year, 1914, was dry the company did very well, but that the year 1915 was a different story. It was rainy—rain almost every day— and the Milk River Flats became a virtual sea of mud. Jack Galbreath, who owned an eight-horse team, camped on this flat that summer and pulled the cars through the mud, which sometimes came up almost to the doors of those open-sided White buses. The sidehill sections were as slick as grease and the vehicles often spent as much time off the road as on it. This period developed a group of exceedingly skillful drivers but sorely taxed the patience and ingenuity of the owner, Mr. Emery. It is to his credit that he stayed with the job and continued to develop the company toward its present-day organization. But those who experienced these years of trial will not soon forget them.

Before long gravel was placed on the surface of this road and the worst sections repaired so that bad weather would not be too much of a hindrance, but repairs and maintenance were carried on continually. The Great Northern, in order to keep these eastside roads and trails available for the necessary visitor travel, continued to spend a considerable amount of money for maintenance, some of which was returned to them later by the Federal Government as funds were made available for this purpose. It is to the everlasting credit of these pioneer concessioners and the far-sightedness of Mr. Hill of the Great Northern Railway that visitor accommodations and transportation facilities were made available to people on the eastern slopes of the park in such a short time. Appropriations to administer the park were very limited and hard to obtain, and had this development been obliged to wait for the Federal funds, it would have been many years making its appearance.

The eastside road from the railhead at Midvale to Many Glacier, with the necessary side roads to Two Medicine and Cutbank Chalets, continued to serve the visitor for many years. Then, in 1924, action was initiated for the construction of a hardsurfaced road from Glacier Park Station to the Canadian boundary, a distance of approximately fifty-four miles. This road along with the necessary feeder roads into the park constituted what is now known as the Blackfeet Highway.

Work on the Blackfeet Highway itself, started in 1926 by the Bureau of Public Roads with 100% federal-aid money, continued to completion in 1929. The Two Medicine Road was constructed between 1925 and 1929, and the Babb-Many Glacier reconstruction was completed with the opening of the bridge at the outlet of Swiftcurrent Lake in 1930. Then, for the first time, the red buses were able to forget the ever-present threat of mud and slippery roads on their daily run from Glacier Park Station.

The only remaining section of the eastside highway system was the so-called "Kennedy Creek Cutoff," later renamed the "Chief Mountain International Highway." Major construction was started on this in 1934 and it was opened to travel on June 14, 1936, although the surfacing was not completed at this time. This highway afforded the first direct connection between Glacier National Park and its sister area, Waterton Lakes National Park, immediately across the border in Alberta. Now this is one of the popular drives from either park and a main route of travel for people crossing the border in the summer months.

Let us pause and take a look at the transportation picture as it existed at the time of the completion of the Blackfeet Highway on the east side in 1929. Here we have a rugged mountain range, crossed at Marias Pass by the railroad, and at various places along its length by trails. A surfaced road leads north from the railroad at Glacier Park Station to the Canadian boundary, with short feeder roads into the lower east side valleys.

On the west side a road extended up the North Fork of the Flathead and construction crews pushed toward the summit of Logan Pass on the Going-to-the-Sun Road. However, travel from one side of the park to the other had to be transported on railroad cars between Belton and Glacier Park Station; hence there was very little of what we now call "transcontinental travel" through the park.

This situation complicated even the administration of the park so that a sub-headquarters was set up at Glacier Park Station to administer the eastern slopes, thereby effectively cutting the area in two. A warehouse, machine shop and the other necessary offices were established there at the location of the present Glacier Park Ranger Station, in East Glacier Park.

By June 20, 1930, the last two contracts for U. S. Highway 2 across the mountains immediately south of the park were completed and the "Roosevelt Highway" was officially opened for travel on July 19, with dedication ceremonies at Marias Pass on August 23. For the first time a coast-to-coast route was opened through the area, allowing more visitors to reach the park without having to back-track to get back on the main routes of travel. This road also made the administration of the park more simple and made available for the first time a much wider use of automobiles by the National Park Service.

GOING-TO-THE-SUN ROAD

The Going-to-the-Sun Road, named by Park Naturalist George C. Ruhle in 1929, is the only trans-mountain road within the boundaries of the park. It gives the visitor who is unable to get into the back country on the trails, a cross section of the beauties and scenery offered by the higher peaks and passes in the range, a view marred only by the man-made scars necessary for such an accomplishment. This road, extending from West Glacier at the western entrance to St. Mary on the eastern side, is a marvel of engineering accomplishment. This wide, two-laned, surfaced road was literally carved out of the precipitous rock mountainsides for approximately twelve miles of its fifty-mile length. This road crosses the Continental Divide on Logan Pass at an elevation of 6,664 feet, a rise of approximately 3,000 feet in elevation in the last nine miles of the climb up the west side.

From the time the park was established, various park superintendents had recommended a trans-mountain road, their interest motivated by a desir for easier administration as well as by the feasibility of a scenic route fo the visitors to travel. As a result of these requests, in 1916 T. Warren Allen an engineer for the Bureau of Public Roads, was sent to make a reconnaissanc of the desired route over the mountains, and in so doing became the firs engineer to make a report upon the feasibility of such a road. As a resul of his report, preliminary surveys were made in 1917 and 1918, following th same route as the present road as far as Trapper (Logan) Creek. From ther the original survey followed up Trapper Creek directly toward the summi of Logan Pass, using a minimum grade of eight per cent (as compared to the present average of five and one-half per cent) on a series of fifty-foot radius switchbacks. Under this survey, Congress, in 1921, appropriated the first money for construction, a total of $100,000, to be expended under contracts on the section from the foot to the head of Lake McDonald, including a spur to the present Lake McDonald Ranger Station.

Further preliminary survey work was carried on in 1918; and in 1919 the first actual work was done on the road by John E. Lewis, owner of the Lewis Hotel at the head of Lake McDonald. He spent over $3,000 that summer cutting three and one-half miles of right-of-way along Lake McDonald, grading two miles of road and building three bridges. His work continued through 1920, but was necessarily slow because of the lack of proper equipment.

On August 16, 1921, the first actual construction contract, other than that done by John Lewis, in the mid-1890's, was awarded for completion of this section to the head of Lake McDonald, under the original $100,000 appropriation. By the summer of 1922, this section was cleared and graded; and in July another contract was awarded for seven additional miles, carrying the road to Avalanche Creek by 1924. This was the end of the road for several years, as far as visitor traffic was concerned, but with the development of the camping area there, many people visited this spot and the nearby Avalanche Lake.

Further appropriations in 1923-24 enabled work to be started on the eastern end of the road, from St. Mary almost to (Going-to-the-Sun) Sun Point, as well as on the section between Avalanche campground and Logan Creek, at the foot of the pass. The contractor on this latter section, however, did not complete his contract as specified, and the National Park Service was forced to take over and complete the job on a force-account basis.

Not being satisfied with the surveyed location of the road up Logan Creek, Park Superintendent Kraebel and Director Mather persuaded the Bureau of Public Roads to re-survey the entire route between the completed portions. In September 1924, Engineer Frank A. Kittridge of the Bureau was put in charge of this survey. During that fall, Kittridge and his crew went over the entire route, fighting bad weather, storms and icy cliffs until the middle of November. Before spring the job was approved on Kittridge's (present) location and bids were let for construction of the remaining twelve miles to the pass from the west side.

During this same winter, 1924-25, the National Park Service and the Bureau of Public Roads reached an agreement whereby the Bureau took over the engineering supervision of this entire construction job. From year to year more and more of the construction supervision on park roads was taken over by the Bureau. By the summer of 1927 practically all of the park road construction program had been placed in their charge.

With the taking over of construction by the Bureau of Public Roads, a decision was reached that all funds would be spent on the west side, as far as was practical to do so, in order to complete the road to Logan Pass in the shortest possible time. By this time there were nine miles completed on the east side and eighteen and one-half miles on the west side, leaving an uncompleted gap between Logan Creek and the vicinity of (Going-to-the-Sun) Sun Point.

The final section on the west side, from Logan Creek to the summit of Logan Pass, was the most difficult section of the entire road. This section was awarded for $869,145, or approximately $71,000 per mile, not including the surfacing and further guardrail work, which brought the total cost to almost $80,000 per mile. Grading was completed to the pass by October 20, 1928, but the road was not opened to the public until the following summer. During the height of this job the contractor employed an average total of 225 men, operating out of five to six camps, and it was estimated that he used approximately one pound of dynamite for each cubic yard of material removed in construction of this road.

In June of 1929 the road's opening to Logan Pass from the west caused a sudden increase in park travel of approximately 18,000 people, most of whom came through the western entrance on their way to the pass. At this time also, Park Naturalist George C. Ruhle suggested the name "Going-to-the-Sun Road" for the new road, a suggestion which was adopted by the National Park Service. With the exception of roadside cleanup, a certain amount of resurfacing, sloping and other relatively minor jobs, the west side road was now completed.

Further contracts were awarded for the uncompleted sections on the eastern slopes of the mountains, and work was carried on toward the road's completion. The last major construction on the road was completed in September 1932, with the exception of the east side tunnel, which was not holed through until October 19. On September 3, 1932, Director Horace Albright headed a party on an inspection tour of the entire road, starting at Lake McDonald Hotel and driving to Logan Pass. From there they proceeded over the construction job to the east side tunnel, as yet unfinished, walked around that to the other end and took another car to the Glacier Park Hotel. Grading was not completed on this last section of the road until the summer of 1933, just in time to let traffic through for the dedication ceremonies.

In order to open the road officially, dedication ceremonies were planned for July 15, 1933, immediately following the opening of the road to public use on July 11. The ceremony was carefully arranged and served to commemorate three events: the opening of the road, the placing of a plaque on Logan Pass in honor of Stephen T. Mather, and the first anniversary of the establishment of the Waterton-Glacier International Peace Park.

DEDICATION CEREMONIES AT LOGAN PASS

The event was attended by nearly 5,000 people, including over 150 Indians of the Blackfeet, Flathead and Kootenai tribes. Among the distinguished guests and speakers were the Governor of Montana, United States Senators Burton K. Wheeler and W. A. Buchanan, and former Congressman Scott Leavitt. Probably the most colorful portion of the ceremony was the part enacted by the Indians, who attended with the intent to affirm a peace between tribes that had formerly been bitter enemies, but which in recent years

DEDICATION CEREMONY AT LOGAN PASS FOR THE OPENING OF THE GOING-TO-THE-SUN ROAD

had let the fires of animosity die without any official sharing of peaceable intentions.

The ardor and sincerity on the part of the Indians was not a bit dampened by an automobile accident on the way to the pass that took the lives of two of their members. At the meeting were many Indian notables, including Kustata, ancient chief of the Kootenais, and eighty-year-old Duncan McDonald, after whom Lake McDonald was named. Also present was Two-Guns White Calf of the buffalo nickel fame and son of the last great chief of the Blackfeet nation. Colorful tepees were erected in the pass to house the Indians who, at the appointed time put on a very colorful and moving pageant depicting the events leading up to this moment, and ending with the smoking of the pipe of peace and the exchanging of gifts, to signify that the tribes were now at peace forever. A more interesting and colorful ceremony has never been enacted within the boundaries of Glacier National Park.

Opening of the road to the public on July 11, 1933, did not mark the end of work to be done on the road, as there still remained to be done a considerable amount of surfacing, re-grading, guardrail installing, roadside clean-up and the like. By the end of 1935 construction costs, from Belton to St. Mary had reached almost $3,000,000, nearly one-third of which was spent on the twelve-mile section between Logan Creek and the summit of the pass. Today when one drives over this road, a modern two-lane roadway literally carved out of solid rock thousands of feet up on a precipitous mountain side, he cannot help but wonder how it was built at any cost.

The Park Trails

Much of this early park history is woven around the use of or search for routes across the mountain range. The old Indian trails were not much as we think of park trails today; but they did follow well-defined routes and were often deeply worn by heavy use. But because of the nature of the terrain and the heavily timbered valleys, trails were almost always a prime necessity if one were to travel from one place to another through these mountain passes.

Very little actual trail construction was undertaken prior to the establishment of the park. We have a record of Mrs. Nat Collins (The Cattle Queen) working the Indian trail over Swiftcurrent Pass in 1883, to make it possible for her pack animals to reach her prospect site on Cattle Queen Creek. Then in 1890 Lieutenant George P. Ahern constructed a trail of sorts to take his party over Ahern Pass; throughout the trip he was cutting out trail in the heavily timbered valleys through which he passed. Dr. Sperry's trail from Lake McDonald to Sperry Glacier and over Gunsight Pass, constructed in 1902 and 1903 by college boys from Minnesota, was probably the first organized trail-building effort in the park.

With the coming of the park, trail building began in earnest, for patrols had to be made, cabins had to be built in the back country, and all the valleys and passes had to be traversed by trails in order to increase the efficient administration of the area as well as to allow park visitors to reach the back country. One of the first bits of reconstruction came about in a rather unusual manner. In May 1910, Chief Clerk Ukker of the Department of the Interior arrived in the park to make an inspection trip and hired Josiah Rogers and his string of horses to pack him through the park. Toward the end of the trip, Ukker expressed a desire to cross Swiftcurrent Pass, which Rogers refused to do that early in the season. After much haggling, Rogers finally consented to take him over, provided that Ukker sign an agreement to pay $100 for each horse lost in the attempt. The details were worked out, the agreement signed, and the party took off for the pass. The trip turned out to be relatively uneventful, but it must have been quite a strain on Ukker's nerves, for upon his return to Washington he set the wheels in motion for reconstruction of this trail. In 1913 it was one of the first trails rebuilt under park appropriations. The new trail consisted of three and one-half miles of switchbacks on the east side of the pass, and was promptly dubbed "Galens Ladder" for James Galen who was then Superintendent of the park. This trail was relocated later, making three routes in all over the pass.

This same summer, work was started on other trails in various sections of the park, pushing on up the valleys and over the passes; by 1918 many of the major trails of today were completed. The Great Northern Railway, in line with its policy of aiding the construction of roads and trails in these early days of the park, also contracted for the building of the Mt. Henry trail, from Glacier Park Station to Two Medicine, in 1913. The area was rapidly being opened up for visitor travel.

One unusual trail-building project that was carried out during this period was that of the Eagle Scout Camps. In 1925 the National Park Service authorized a series of work projects and encampments in the park in which Eagle Scouts, selected from troops throughout the United States, attended a twelve-day encampment and worked on trail-building projects. Captain R. G. Matthews, Scout Executive from Everett, Washington, was in charge of the camps, and the record year, 1930, saw fifty-four scouts from eighteen states enrolled in this project. Starting in 1925, the project continued through 1931, except for 1926, to be financed by the National Park Service. The boys paid their own transportation to and from the park. In 1932 the Park Service was unable to continue the financing and no camps were held. But in 1934 an arrangement was made whereby the boys would finance the project themselves, and the camps were held once again. In 1935 there was a National Scout Jamboree that prevented the boys from returning. This lapse, coupled with financing difficulties, seemed to put a damper on the project, and the camps were given up, never to be resumed. Many miles of good trails were built by these boys, who, at the same time they worked, enjoyed a pleasurable period of camping in the wilderness. Work on the trails amounted to twelve days a year, five hours per day; a good showing was made considering the time spent upon them.

INTERNATIONAL PEACE PARK

Lying as it does immediately adjacent to Waterton Lakes National Park in Canada, the two parks separated only by the thickness of an imaginary boundary line, Glacier National Park cannot be separated geographically from its neighboring recreational area. The two parks are almost identical in significance and were set aside with the same purpose in mind. This unity between the two areas gives both of them an international character that was first recognized by United States Senator Penrose in 1910 when, during the debates on the bill to establish Glacier National Park, he stated, "This park will be international in character." Recognizing this fact, and wishing to commemorate the friendly relations that existed between the people of the United States and Canada, the combined Rotary Clubs of Montana and Alberta, meeting at the Prince of Wales Hotel in Waterton Park on July 4, 1931, passed a resolution starting the movement for establishment of what was to be known as the "Waterton-Glacier International Peace Park." This was a non-administrative union, aimed at bringing into closer relationships the two parks and their respective nations.

CAIRN DEDICATION

Vigorous action was taken by representatives of Rotary International in both countries, and as a result a bill was introduced into the United States Congress in 1932 by Congressman Scott Leavitt of Montana, to establish this joint park. The bill was passed by both houses and was signed by President Herbert Hoover on December 8, 1932. Similar action was taken in the Canadian Parliament, led by Premier Brounler, Brigadier General Steward, and Mr. Lethbridge, making the joint park a reality.

In 1947 a cairn was built on each side of the Canadian boundary, at the Chief Mountain Customs, commemorating the establishment of this joint park. Appropriate cornerstone laying and dedication ceremonies were held by Rotary Clubs and officials of both parks, dedicating these monuments for all time to the friendly relationship that exists between these two nations.

CIVILIAN PUBLIC WORKS PROGRAM
Civilian Conservation Corps

One of President Franklin D. Roosevelt's first acts after he took office

CCC CAMP NO. 3

97

for the first time was to tackle the problem of acute unemployment. This problem was particularly serious among the young men of the cities and towns throughout the United States, who could not compete for jobs with the men who had families to support. As part of his program to solve this unemployment, on March 31, 1933, Congress passed an act authorizing the establishment of a program of public works for these young men in National Forests and National Parks. Under this program termed "Emergency Conservation Work" the Civilian Conservation Corps was set up.

During the months of May and June 1933, eight so-called "CCC" camps were established in the park, each consisting of from fifty to two hunded and fifty men. The boys, mostly teen-age, were under the supervision of Army officers in camp and under civilian foremen and supervisors on the job. The first month was spent in camp construction, followed by increasing amounts of fieldwork, mainly involving cleanup of the burned area of the fire of 1929 in the southwestern corner of the park. This program continued to grow as work was laid out for them, and before long these crews became the mainstay of the park labor organization. Fourteen different campsites were located within the park along with numerous "spike" camps for small work crews. One of the biggest jobs carried out by these crews was the cleanup after the 1929 and 1936 forest fires, in which over 12,000 acres of unsightly snags were felled, cut up into wood or lumber, and removed from the area. Six and one-half miles of lead-covered telephone cable was carried in and laid down over Logan Pass, all by hand, for the first trans-mountain telephone cable installation. Over 150 acres of campground sites were prepared for use and many miles of roadside cleanup accomplished. Buildings, trails, roads, and telephone lines were constructed and maintained throughout the park. Sewer and water systems were installed, enlarged, or repaired. These and thousands of other jobs were accomplished by these boys in the years they were in the park—many of them jobs that could not have been accomplished otherwise because of the high costs involved.

One of the CCC's biggest values to the park, as well as to other forested areas, was in fire-suppression work. Hundreds of thousands of hours were spent by these crews in suppressing forest fires, at times when civilian crews were not available in sufficient numbers or in time to do any good. Trained crews were stationed at various areas on other work projects, with their tools ready for instant getaway in case of fire call, and it was not unusual to see a twenty-five- or fifty-man crew on the way to a fiire within five minutes following the first call.

During the latter part of the CCC period crews were cut down until there were only two camps in the park, both located near Belton (West Glacier). After the entrance of the United States into World War II all CCC projects were halted and the last camp, NP-9, was evacuated on July 17, 1942, ending the CCC program in the park.

Emergency Relief Act.

Another emergency agency originating from the depression years that located in the park was a branch of the Works Progress Administration, authorized under the "Emergency Relief Act." Under this act, a camp of loggers and others from the relief rolls was set up at the mouth of the North Fork of the Flathead River and assigned to fire hazard reduction work along the park boundary of the 1929 fire area. These crews, recruited from local communities, felled the snags and cleaned up all dead timber on a wide strip along the boundary of the park in the vicinity of the Flathead River Ranger Station. Posts, telephone poles and wood were salvaged as far as was practical, and the remainder piled and burned. This program was carried on through the years of 1938 and up to November 25, 1939, when all ERA activity was closed down in the park with the exception of a few essential personnel left to clean up the accounting and property records.

Civilian Public Service

The third group of public works crews assigned to the park was the Civilian Public Service organization, composed of conscientious objectors, members of religious groups that did not believe in carrying arms during time of war. On about September 15, 1942, the first of this group of men began to arrive, to fix up the old CCC camp NP-9 for occupancy by those to follow. By the end of the month there were around one hundred and twenty-five men in camp; the number of men in the park for the duration of the camp stayed at approximately that figure.

Foremen, mechanics, and a camp superintendent were appointed and these crews immediately started to work on projects of operation and maintenance that were to keep the park functioning during the war years. With the heavy drain of manpower because of the war, these men were an invaluable aid to the maintenance and protection of the park, particularly in the field of fire protection, since trained crews were just not available otherwise.

This program continued through most of 1946, diminishing in numbers steadily toward the end, until, on September 30, 1946, the camp was closed, leaving only a few people behind to close up camp and turn the records over to the proper authorities.

THREATS TO THE UNITY OF THE PARK

Glacier View Dam

The most serious threat to the unity of Glacier National Park that has made its appearance was the proposal to build a dam on the North Fork of the Flathead River near Glacier View Mountain, with the resulting threat of flooding of thousands of acres of land in the northwestern area of the park. As part of the proposed development of the Columbia River Basin for increased water power, the Army Engineers and the Bonneville Power Administration began to look toward the upper reaches of the streams for power and storage development. The first of these proposals investigated was the raising of Flathead Lake by several feet to increase the capacity of the Polson power plant and provide additional downriver storage. When this proposal was brought up in 1942, it created a storm of protest from the local citizens who stood in danger of losing lands by flooding or raising the water level. Hearings to allow the people to express their opinions upon this were held, at which time alternate sites for water storage were suggested, including the damsite at Glacier View Mountain.

Preliminary surveys were made of various sites for dams along the North Fork of the Flathead by the Army Corps of Engineers. In 1944 and 1945, with the permission of the Department of the Interior, test drilling was carried on at two sites, Glacier View and Foolhen Hill, both on the North Fork along the Park boundary. As a result of these surveys and the furor over the raising of Flathead Lake, public opinion in some of the neighboring towns began to crystallize in favor of building the dam at Glacier View, to which plan the National Park Service objected very strongly.

Pressure for the building of the Glacier View Dam mounted rapidly under favorable reports by the Army Engineers of its feasibility. The National Park Service took an equally strong position against its construction, until, on May 25, 1948, a public hearing was held in Kalispell by the Army Engineers to allow the people again to air their views. This hearing was attended by representatives of all the agencies concerned, as well as by many private citizens. By this time the question had blossomed out as a national issue and the National Park Service, backed by most of the nation's conservation organizations, was making an all-out drive to have the issue defeated. The Army Engineers, on the other hand, backed by certain local groups, were pressing for the dam's construction. By 1949 the issue had reached a point where the Secretaries of War and the Interior were forced to step in and take a hand. The two men met, after considering all points for and against the dam, reached an agreement that it would not be built without the full consent of both departments. This effectively stopped the threat of Glacier View Dam for the time being; since that time, however, there have been several minor threats of the dam's reoccurrence, including a bill introduced into Congress.

Alienated Lands Within the Park

Another major problem in park administration, one that has been in existence since 1910, is the fact that there were several thousand acres of private and state lands within the park boundaries. These lands, as a whole, did not constitute a great threat to the park, yet from time to time situations arose in connection with them that seriously threatened park values. For that reason the National Park Service has for many years been carrying on a program of buying up such lands as they become available. This is a slow process, and one that requires more and more funds as time goes on and the lands increase in value.

The problem of private lands originated with the homesteading of the area and the staking of mining claims prior to the turn of the century. When the park was established there was a considerable number of such homesteads and claims, some of which were of considerable size. The act which created the park recognized the rights of ownership of this property and granted the holders full use and enjoyment of it, within the limits of park rules and regulations. The mining claims were located mostly on the eastern slopes of the mountains, mainly in the Many Glacier Valley. Action by the General Land Office in the 1920's cleared most of them off the records, because of lack of evidence of assessment work or mineral veins. A few mines were patented though, and are still in private hands or have been purchased by the park. The lack of paying mineral veins in the area prevents these claims from being a major threat to park values except where they might be located in areas suitable for other types of development.

The homesteads and summer homes are located mainly on the west side of the park, principally along the North Fork of the Flathead River and around Lake McDonald. These lands have changed hands frequently, and from time to time cabin camps, eating places and stores have been built upon them for the accommodation of park visitors. As the demand for summer homesites increased, the value of property in choice locations increased to the point where it was impractical for the Federal Government to purchase it, but other properties have occasionally become available for purchase and have been gradually added to the public land area. In this connection the Glacier Natural History Association was formed, as an incorporated organization functioning solely for the park interest, and part of whose funds were set aside for the purchase of private lands within the park. This fund was built up by donations from interested persons and used to purchase tax title to private lands, or other acquisitions that the government was unable to make, and hold these lands until title was cleared and the government could repurchase it. This plan greatly facilitated the acquisition of property within the park by having a revolving fund readily accessible, and has resulted in a considerable number of private land purchases that would otherwise have been impossible.

The third, and until recently the most controversial, group of alienated lands in the park was a group of holdings, mainly on the North Fork of the Flathead, owned by the State of Montana and totalling over 10,000 acres. These holdings came into being, after the area was set aside as a park, through a series of negotiations and exchanges between the National Park Service and the State of Montana whereby certain sections of land within the boundaries of the park were transferred to the State by the Federal Government. These holdings were in lieu of loss to the state grant for common school and capital building purposes by reason of the establishment of the park. The period from 1911 into the early 1920's was spent in making these substitute selections; there is no record of any attempt by the State to sell or the Federal Government to repurchase them. The first recorded mention of any transfer of these lands back to the park occurred on April 11, 1924, when State Forester McLaughlin wrote to Superintendent Kraebel suggesting the exchange of certain state lands within the park for forested lands of equal value outside. Negotiations were started, mainly with the United States Forest Service, and a few exchanges were made; but since the State desired forested lands, and the Forest Service did not agree to the exchanges, negotiations came to a halt in 1929. Except for futile efforts to reach an agreement between the various parties involved, little was done until the late 1940's when efforts were again made to find lands that were suitable for exchange. As the Forest Service did not wish to exchange their lands, and the National Park Service did not have funds for outright purchase, attention was finally turned toward exchange of lands administered under the Taylor Grazing Act. Here again an impasse resulted. Then a series of meetings during 1948 resulted in a plan whereby the Federal Government would furnish funds for fifty per cent, the total to be placed in the public school and capital building fund. This idea was meeting with some favor when the state elections changed the administration and put an entirely different approach to the situation.

The new State administration soon precipitated a crisis by offering for sale the timber on certain of these lands, and actually did sell the timber from one section of 640 acres. This stirred up conservation agencies and newspapers throughout the state and the matter was brought to a head, with representatives of both State and Federal Government pitching in to find a solution. Enabling legislation was passed by both the State and Federal legislatures, and finally, on February 28,1953. Governor J. Hugo Aronson signed Senate Bill No. 163, enacted by the 33rd session of the Montana Legislature, approving the exchange of these lands for lands of equal value in eastern Montana which were then managed by the Bureau of Land Management.

On July 18, 1953, a ceremony was held in the park to dedicate this exchange of lands and to celebrate the end of the long drawn-out struggle. Attending the ceremony were Secretary of the Interior Douglas McKay, Director of the National Park Service Conrad Wirth, Regional Director Howard Baker, Governor J. Hugo Aronson of Montana, and other dignitaries, including Superintendent J. W. Emmert who had taken the lead locally for the National Park Service in the later years of the negotiations.

MISSION 66

In the mid-1950's the nation was feeling the spirit of the age of technology. Pulling itself out from an uncomfortable economic recession, self-consciously counting its scientists and mathematicians at the height of the "Cold War," the country devoted itself to a creed of development. At the same time, Americans were also getting their first real taste of the pleasures of increasing leisure time and travel opportunities. These two factors combined to help inspire the National Park Service's Mission 66 Program.

Mission 66 was a ten year program culminating in 1966, dedicated primarily to providing for the ever-increasing public use of National Park Service areas. Based on the prevailing mood in the country, the program's answer to the problems of greater visitation was relatively simple...provide more and improved facilities and services. The theme was public exposure, in volume, to nature's domain (an interesting contrast to the protectionist conservatism to come in the '70s). This is not to say that there was no regard for protecting the environment, but rather that the threat of man's abuse was not seen to be as significant as the growing public pressure on apparently inadequate park facilities.

Virtually all areas of Glacier were affected during this era. Campgrounds, roads, trails, administrative buildings, employee quarters, visitor centers, interpretive programs, and even concession operations were all expanded and improved. Some of the more outstanding projects are worth mentioning in some detail.

Fish Creek Campground was developed to include 180 sites, and at the lower end of St. Mary Lake a completely new 156-site campground was created.

At Park Headquarters the log administration building which had served superintendents and their staff since 1924 was finally retired in 1962 and replaced with a large, modern, three-story structure. In the same year two eight-unit apartment buildings were constructed, one at Headquarters and one at St. Mary, culminating a program of employee quarters construction which had erected many modern, ranch-style houses in the park in the 1950s.

The most prominent feature of expanded interpretive activities was the construction of visitor centers at Logan Pass and at St. Mary. Both were opened and dedicated in 1966. The Logan Pass Visitor Center was at the hub of visitor activities at the pass with the Sun Road and two trails spreading out like spokes, and naturalist programs were created to center on the new facility.

The most prominent road construction during this period was the Camas Creek Road extending approximately ten miles northwest from Apgar to and crossing the North Fork of the Flathead River.

NATURE PREDOMINATES

The features of Glacier National Park are treasured for their majesty. Visitors come, at least in part, to witness the awesomeness of nature. Yet many are apparently impressed only in a static sense, as by an overwhelming painting or photograph. In the 1960's, however, nature seemed determined to remind man that an awesome environment breeds awesome events. It was almost as if she had decided to humble man after his decade of great technological achievements.

The 1964 seasonal activity started like most other years. In May, park lakes opened to fishing and road crews were busy clearing snow and patching holes. The forks of the Flathead River were rising, as usual, with run-off from mountain snows, and the Hungry Horse News reported that river conditions late in the month were setting "a good pattern for a safe runoff" (Hungry Horse News, page 1, 5/22/64). On the 21st the flood gauge at Columbia Falls measured 12.4 feet of water...flood stage being 14 feet and damage starting after 15 feet. "Nearly every spring sees the river top 12.0 feet on the Columbia Falls gauge" the News noted. Then the weather cooled, slowing runoff and concern over the river dropped with its level.

Up on the Sun Road in early June, bulldozers were pushing through the giant drifts as they did each year, clearing Logan Pass. But nature was warming up for summer with her own routine, and this year it included a heart-stopping practical joke on the men high on the Divide. Four park maintenance men were putting two bulldozers to the task of cutting the deep drifts. Charles Siderius was carefully maneuvering his 25-ton machine when he heard "a loud rifle-like cracking noise, louder than the cat engine." Beneath him a slab of snow three feet deep and nearly an acre in area suddenly started to tumble down the 45 degree slope. Siderius instantly decided to hold on and ride it out. The mass of snow rumbled downward, tossing the dozer and its passenger in six complete rolls on its way. Finally they stopped, 350 feet below the road. The machine was upside down and all that could be seen of Siderius was his right hand above the snow. The others rushed down, turned off the running engine, and heard a voice say, "Get the snow off my head so I can breathe!" Siderius was quickly uncovered and rushed to the Kalispell Hospital where the fortunate operator was found to have suffered only a couple fractured ribs at worst. Two days later, while he was still recuperating, his dozer was back at work with the crew clearing the road. Nature had taken her warm-up exercises.

In the next few days the cool spell that had slowed spring's arrival dissipated. Warm weather melted the snows, streams swelled, and on June 4 the river gauge at Columbia Falls once again recorded a moderate 12.0 feet. Rain came on the 6th and continued for three days. By mid-day on Monday, the 8th, the waters were at flood stage, 14 feet. By 8:00 p.m. the gauge read 18 fe. Upstream bridges were cracking and slumping, Nyack was inundated, and power and water were off at West Glacier. At 11:00 p.m. the river rose over the top of the gauge at 20.4 feet. U.S. Highway 2 and the Great Northern Railroad were being devoured in large peices by the Middle Fork of the Flathead River. Lower McDonald Creek had reversed its flow and poured into Lake McDonald instead of out of it, propelled by the incredible volume of water. At 11:30 a.m. on Tuesday the 9th, the raging mass of water crested at an unimaginable 26 feet, then began to recede.

The 1964 flood was the worst in Montana's history and the destruction caused was nearly beyond belief. Downstream, large sections of Kalispell were damaged, including about 2500 homes. Serious flooding also hit other communities in the area, and seven counties of northwestern Montana were declared a disaster area by President Lyndon Johnson. Miraculously no deaths resulted from the torrent within the park; however numerous persons lost their lives on the Blackfeet Reservation.

At Glacier National Park the western side of the Divide was hardest hit and in fact was physically isolated for a time, as all connecting bridges were damaged beyond use. At Polebridge the western end of the bridge was unusable. Farther south, at the junction of the North and Middle Fork, the Blankenship Bridge was washed out (the Camas Creek Road bridge over the North Fork had not yet been built). In West Glacier the steel bridge built in 1938 was pounded by logs and debris until it buckled and sagged. A few hundred yards up the Middle Fork the 1919 bridge which had served the park in its earliest days was swept away, leaving only the supporting concrete arch. Still farther up, along U.S. Highway 2 at the Walton Ranger Station, yet another bridge was destroyed. Within the park the waters also raged. Upper McDonald Creek tore away a log bridge. The lake itself, fed for a time from both ends, surrounded government and private buildings in Apgar and swamped Sprague Creek Campground. Sprague Creek itself also helped fill the campground with debris and not far away Snyder Creek took away part of the dining room at Lake McDonald Lodge. Lower McDonald Creek, flowing first one way and then the other, destroyed a number of private cabins. Across the Divide the most serious damage was experienced at St. Mary, where Divide Creek filled the community with water.

A year later reconstruction work would still be patching up after the flood. But within a month after the disaster Glacier was operating in a remarkably normal fashion. The 1919 bridge in West Glacier was temporarily rebuilt on its concrete arch to handle traffic, while the larger bridge was being replaced. The Going-to-the-Sun Road had escaped major damage and quickly took the place of U.S. Highway 2 and the railroad, both closed, in handling travel across the Divide. While northwestern Montana struggled to recover during the summer of 1964, the park served more than 640,000 visitors in a manner approaching "business as usual."

The forces of nature rested in the year 1965. Northwest Montana continued to clean up from the year before, and its people sighed in tentative relief. But in an area where the natural environment and its natural inhabitants predominate over man and his creations, complacency and routine have no place. Residents were soon rudely reminded of that fact. Almost two years to the day after the rains that brought terrible destruction, a freak storm hit the park and surrounding country. On June 3 and 4 clouds suddenly released precipitation that amounted to as much as three inches of rain in Kalispell and five inches of wet snow in the park and Whitefish Where snow accumulated, trees, utility poles, and wires were broken and tangled. Most of Glacier National Park was temporarily without power, as were nearby communities. Damage was soon repaired, but man had been reminded of his place. Natural events continued to dominate the most recent history of the park.

A year later in the summer of 1967 the freak snow that had created such havoc would now have been a welcome relief from the warm, dry weather, which was creating the greatest fire threat in years. By late July there had been eleven fires, most caused by lightning. Although these fires had been small, the danger was rated as "very high" to "extreme." In the first half of the month Glacier was fighting 17 fires concurrently with 700 men from throughout Montana and other national parks. The largest fire covered about 600 acres on Huckleberry Mountain, while the second largest consumed 400 acres of Glacier Wall opposite the Garden Wall and Going-to-the-Sun Road. Both of these fires and most of the others were started by a lightning storm on August 11.

On August 23, while hundreds of men struggled to contain it, high winds whipped up the Huckleberry fire, sweeping it across the new Camas Road and up the park side of the North Fork, over an area of 2400 acres. The same winds also spread the Glacier Wall fire to 700 acres. Over 1200 men were now on the scene in the park.

In the last days of August, fire control officials finally announced that all blazes were under control. Manpower and equipment were cut back while "mop up" operations continued. The Huckleberry fire had burned 8400 acres and on Glacier Wall, 700 acres. Then suddenly on September 1 the winds rose again even higher than before. The Huckleberry fire was still in check, but in the McDonald Valley the Glacier Wall fire jumped the firelines, rushed across the creek and up the Garden Wall fire jumped the firelines, rushed across the creek and up the Garden Wall and 700 men were again brought into the effort. By the 4th, the fire was contained once and for all, but not before it scorched 3110 acres of forest.

Park officials later reported that the battle against the flames in 1967 had involved 1650 men, 12 helicopters, eight airplanes, and 22 bulldozers, and that more than 12,000 acres had been consumed in fire. In area affected, it was the largest fire year since 1929, and fourth largest in park history.

GRIZZLIES AND TRAGEDY

Every summer dozens of high school and college students come to Glacier to work for the concessioners and most spend their spare time exploring the wonders of the park. On the evening of August 12, 1967, Roy Ducat, age 18, and Julie Helgeson, age 19, both employees of Glacier Park, Inc., were camping at Granite Park near the Chalet. Five other employees, including Michele Koons, 19, were in a separate group camped at Trout Lake, miles away. After midnight a sow grizzly with two cubs wandered about the Granite Park area and suddenly at about 12:45 a.m., the sow attacked Ducat and Helgeson in their sleeping bags. In a few minutes the bear was gone, the girl was dead, and Ducat badly hurt. At Trout Lake a lone sow grizzly marauded the campsite during the day and returned at 2:00 a.m. to harass the five as they slept. Finally she attacked Michele Koons, ultimately killing her.

The tragic story made national headlines and later became the subject of a best selling book, "Night of the Grizzlies." These were the first fatalities resulting from encounters with bears in the park's history and in fact significant incidents with bears had been recorded only since 1941. It was now apparent that increased visitor use of the backcountry was directly related to such incidents and an effective bear management plan was in order. Such a plan was quickly and carefully created. It combined old techniques, such as relocating or destroying problem bears, with new ideas, including packing out all garbage (eliminating backcountry garbage dumps such as existed at Granite Park), extensive education of visitors and employees regarding bears, criminal citation of visitors feeding bears, and sign-in registers at trailheads. Bear management is now a regular aspect of visitor protection policies and ranger activities.

THE '70S

The most prominent events of the 1970s are still to be written. It remains to be seen whether man or nature will dominate this decade in the park. But it is certain that the public mood and Park Service philosophies have changed significantly since Mission 66 and are directed more than ever toward protecting the environment from overwhelming visitor use. At Glacier this will probably be revealed in efforts to control the use of private motor vehicles and in a "freeze" on visitor facilities such as formal campgrounds and concession operation. At the same time vastly increased use of the backcountry for hiking, camping, skiing, and mountaineering are requiring new directions in policies and activities. The history of the '70s, then, will probably reflect the great challenge of unprecedented use of the park by the American public.

SNYDER CREEK. The stream changed its course in many places. Trees were uprooted and the stream bed scoured. Many creeks have not yet stabilized. These are natural processes.

APPENDIX A

HISTORIC PLACE NAMES

Some of the most interesting history of Glacier National Park is connected with the origin of its place names. The majority of the park features were named in the early days when the first exploration and mapping were carried on, between 1880 and 1910. Often these features were named for some noted person or for some event that occurred at that place. George Bird Grinnell and James Willard Schultz are responsible for the predominance of Indian names given to many of the peaks on the eastern side of the park prior to 1900. Dr. George C. Ruhle in 1938 and 1939 also renamed many of the park features with either their original Indian names or names that honored some particular Indian.

The following is by no means the complete list, but includes those names of historical interest and those of which the origin of the name is not readily apparent.

ADAIR RIDGE — Named for W. L. (Billy) Adair, an old timer who settled on a homestead on Adair Ridge and later ran the store at Polebridge, Montana.

AGASSIZ GLACIER (Creek)—Named for the noted Swiss-American zoologist, geologist and scientist, Louis J. R. Agassiz.

AHERN PASS (Creek, Glacier, Peak) — Named for Lieutenant George P. Ahern who, with a detachment of Negro soldiers from the 25th Infantry, crossed this pass in August 1890. This was the first known successful attempt to take pack stock over Ahern Pass.

AKOKALA CREEK (Lake) — Kootenai name meaning "rotten." The creek was formerly known as "Indian Creek," and the lake as "Oil Lake."

ALLEN MOUNTAIN (Creek)—Named for Cornelia Seward Allen, wife of F. T. Allen of New York, granddaughter of Wm. H. Seward, Secretary of State under Abraham Lincoln.

ALMOST-A-DOG MOUNTAIN — Almost-A-Dog was a Blackfeet Indian, one of the few survivors of the Baker Massacre of January 23, 1870.

ALTYN PEAK—This name was given by the miners in the late 1890's to the mountain we now know as Mt. Wynn. As G. B. Grinnell had previously called the latter "Point Mountain," topographers later transferred the name to the peak to which it is now applied. A U. S. Geological Survey map of 1912 also shows this peak as "McDermott Peak." The name "Altyn" was taken from the little mining town of Altyn that was situated near the head of Sherburne Lake, which, in turn, received its name from Dave Greenwood Altyn, one of the financial backers of the Cracker Lake Mine.

106

APGAR VILLAGE (Mountain)—Named for Dimon Apgar, one of the early settlers who came to the foot of Lake McDonald prior to 1900 and built a home and cabins at the site of the present village of Apgar.

APPEKUNNY MOUNTAIN (Creek, Falls)—The Indian name for George Willard Schultz, meaning "White-spotted Robe," or "Scabby Robe," that is, one that was badly tanned, leaving hard spots. Schultz was a white who married into the Blackfeet tribe and lived with them for many years. He was a close friend of George Bird Grinnell and wrote stories of Indian life for Grinnell's magazine as well as several books.

APPISTOKI PEAK (Creek, Falls)—Named by R. T. Evans, a topographer who worked on the early map of the park. It is reported that he inquired from his Indian guide what word the Blackfeet used for "looking over something," and the guide, misunderstanding the meaning of his question, gave him the name "Appistoki," for the Indian god who looks over everything and everyone.

ATSINA LAKE (Falls) — The Blackfeet name for their allies, the Gros Ventre tribe.

AURICE LAKE—For Mrs. Aurice Houston, wife of Dr. Roderick Houston, a retired dentist who took up a homestead at the foot of Lake McDonald and operated a cabin camp there until his death in 1950. "Doc" Houston was a noted fishing guide and took fishing parties down the rivers adjacent to the park until just prior to his death.

AVALANCHE LAKE (Creek)—Named by Dr. Lyman B. Sperry in 1895 on his first trip into the area, because of the large avalanche tracks down the walls of the basin surrounding the lake.

BARING CREEK (Falls)—Named for one of the Baring brothers, London bankers who were guided on a hunting trip into the area in the late 1880's by Joe Kipp and James Willard Schultz.

BELLY RIVER — The origin of this name is quite debatable, and several sources of it have been presented. The "Glacier National Park Drivers' Manual" presents the most complete story of these varied origins: "The origin of the name is in dispute, although the Belly River, the Gros Ventre Indians, and the Big Belly Buttes upon the river between Cardston and MacLeod (Alberta) are connected. One belief is as follows: The Blackfeet people had a custom of apportioning the anatomy of Napi all over the landscape. His elbow was the Bow River at Calgary. His knees were the Teton Buttes. Midway lay his stomach, and what more appropriate than the aforementioned buttes, which to the Indian resembled the contorted manifold of a buffalo. Hence, they became Mokowanis, or Big Belly Buttes. The river that flowed at their base became Mokowanis River, and later, when Indians from Algonquin nations of the southeast drifted into the region, and established themselves along the river, these too, became Mokowanis or, simply translated into French, the 'Gros Ventres.' Another version has it that the Gros Ventres were so called because they 'eat much and have big paunches.' Certainly their alternative name, Atsina, or Gut People, gives this interpretation support. The river which flowed through their country simply took its name from them. The Arrowsmith map of 1802 called this river Moo-coo-wans, by which name it was sometimes referred to later. On David Thompson's map of 1814, it was marked Stee-muk-ske-picken, signifying Bullhead. The Palliser map of 1865 labeled it Oldman River. The reconnaissance maps of the United States Northern Boundary Commission, 1872-76, labeled it Belly River, which name has been officially adopted by both the United States and Canada.''

BELTON — Believed to have been named ''Bell's Town,'' or ''Belton'' for Daniel Webster Bell, who took up a claim near the townsite at the time of the construction of the Great Northern Railway and cut ties for the railroad. He was a Civil War veteran and served as cook for the location parties of the Great Northern in 1890.

BLACKFOOT GLACIER (Mountain) — This glacier was discovered and named for the Blackfeet Indians by George Bird Grinnell on a trip to the head of the St. Mary Valley in 1891. This glacier was called ''Old Man Ice,'' by the Kootenai Indians, Red Eagle Glacier was ''Old Woman Ice,'' Sperry Glacier was ''Son Ice,'' and Pumpelly Glacier was ''Daughter Ice.''

BOWMAN LAKE (Creek) — Believed to have been named for Fred Bowman, a trapper who came to Montana from Wyoming in 1885 and started to trap on the North Fork of the Flathead, in the area surrounding Bowman Lake.

BROWN, MT. — Named for William Brown of Chicago, then Solicitor General for the Chicago and Alton Railroad, by some members of his party on a camping and fishing trip to the area around Lake McDonald in 1894. The companions, Charles H. Russell (not the artist) and Frank A. Johnson, climbed this mountain that arose back of their camp, and so named it.

BROWN PASS — Named for John George (Kootenai) Brown, the first superintendent of Waterton Lakes National Park, who is reported to have used this pass on his first trip into the Waterton Lakes area from California.

CALF ROBE MOUNTAIN — Named for a Blackfeet Indian, who, legend relates, had a weird and unusual experience with a grizzly bear. Calf Robe was deserted by his fellow warriors in enemy country and left to die; but he was soon rescued by a large grizzly bear, who brought him food and carried him to help near Fort Benton. This incident is supposed to have happened about 1870.

CAMERON LAKE — Named for D. R. Cameron, British Commissioner with the International Boundary Commission.

CAMPBELL MOUNTAIN — Some sources state that Campbell was a member of the Boundary Survey party, but James Willard Schultz attributes the name to Supt. F. C. Campbell, of the Blackfeet Indian Reservation.

CANNON, MT. — Named for a young couple who spent their honeymoon in this region and climbed this mountain. Dr. L. B. Sperry originally named it "Goat Mountain" in 1894.

CAPER PEAK — Named by Surveyor R. T. Evans, who is reported to have counted over 30 goats "capering" on this peak.

CARCAJOU LAKE — Named for a mythical being of the Cree Indians, meaning "hungry," or "eats a lot," and from which the English word "carcajou," for wolverine, is derived.

CARTER GLACIER (Mountain) — For Senator T. H. Carter of Montana, who introduced into the United States Senate the bill that established Glacier National Park.

CATTLE QUEEN CREEK — Mrs. Nat Collins, a woman known as the "Cattle Queen of Montana" ran a cattle ranch near the present town of Choteau, Montana, prior to 1900, and had a mining claim along this creek which she worked for several years.

CHANEY GLACIER — Named after Professor L. W. Chaney of Carleton College, Northfield, Minnesota, by Dr. Lyman B. Sperry. Dr. Chaney was a geologist on one of Dr. Sperry's parties into the McDonald Valley in 1895, on which trip they penetrated this wilderness to the summit of the Garden Wall and actually went out upon this glacier.

CHAPMAN PEAK — Named for Robert H. Chapman, of the Geological Survey, one of the topographers who worked on the mapping of the park between 1900 and 1904.

CHIEF MOUNTAIN — This geological oddity, standing as it does on the plains east of the main range, has attracted the attention of explorers and mapmakers from the earliest times. Its existence was first noted on the Arrowsmith maps, published in England in 1795 or 1796, upon which it was called "King Mountain." Peter Fidler, who supplied the information for these maps, visited this area in 1792, and was the first white man to record having seen this landmark. Captain Meriwether Lewis is also believed to have seen the mountain on his trip up the Marias in 1806 and called it "Tower Mountain." James Doty, who explored the eastern front of the range in 1854 for Governor Stevens, reports it as "The Chief or King Mountain." We judge from this that he was referring to it also by the Indian name of "The Chief." There are two records of the origin of another name for this peak — "Kaiser Peak" — by which it was known for some time. Some say it was so-named by early German geographers, but the most authentic story

109

comes from Eli Guardipee, a member of the Blackfeet tribe, who stated that it was so named for a "Bull-whacker" (oxen freighter) named Lee Kaiser, who accidently shot himself near the present town of Cardston, Alberta, in 1872. For him the creek where this happened was known as "Lee Creek," and the mountain at its headwaters was called "Kaiser Peak."

There are many legends regarding this mountain, the most popular being that of the young Flathead Indian brave who spent several days upon the top of the peak searching for his "medicine vision," and using a bison skull for a pillow. When Henry L. Stimson, later Secretary of State, and his companions first climbed to the top of this mountain in 1892, they were probably the first white men to d oso. There they found an ancient bison skull almost entirely decomposed, giving considerable authenticity to this popular legend.

The present name was taken from the Blackfeet Indian name "Old Chief," or "The Mountain-of-the-Chief," by which it was known to the Blackfeet, probably because of the above-mentioned legend.

CLEMENTS MOUNTAIN -- Named by Ross Carter for Walter M. Clements, one of the commissioners who, along with George Bird Grinnell, negotiated with the Blackfeet and consummated the treaty that enabled the Federal Government to purchase the "Ceded Strip" of land that included all of what is now Glacier National Park east of the Continental Divide.

CLEVELAND, MT. — Named by George Bird Grinnell for former President Cleveland. Grinnell first saw it in 1898 from the summit of Blackfoot Mountain, and so named it.

COONSA CREEK — Named for the Indian guide that accompanied John F. Stevens on his exploration into Marias Pass in December, 1889.

CRACKER LAKE — In 1897 two prospectors, L. S. Emmons and Hank Norris, were following a mineral lead through the mountains and stopped on the shore of Cracker Lake (then known as "Blue Lake") for lunch. When they resumed their journey they put their crackers and cheese beneath some rocks, intending to return later and pick them up, which they never did. Thereafter they referred to the mineral lead that they were following as the "lead where we left the crackers," and later as the "Cracker Lead." As this lead passed under the lake, it naturally followed that soon the lake became known as "Cracker Lake."

CROSSLEY LAKE (Ridge) — Named for Joe Cosley (erroneously called Crossley), a half-breed hunter and trapper who often trapped in this area and later served for some time as a park ranger. This lake, along with Glenns Lake, is shown on George Bird Grinnell's 1892 map as "Lansing Lakes."

CUSTER, MT. — Probably named for General George A. Custer, who was killed in the famous Custer Massacre.

CUT BANK CREEK (Pass)—Named for the "cutbanks of white clay along the creek east of Browning. The old Indian name means "Cuts-into-the-white-clay-bank-river."

DAWN MIST FALLS — Probably named for the Indian girl who was the lover of "White Quiver," in the Indian novel by H. F. Sanders. Original name of the falls was "Morning Dew."

DAWSON PASS — Named for Thomas Dawson, an old-time guide in this area, and son of Andrew Dawson, last factor of the American Fur Company at Fort Benton.

DIXON GLACIER — Named for United States Senator Joseph M. Dixon, of Montana, who supported the passage of the bill creating Glacier National Park.

DOODY, MT. — Named for Dan Doody, who trapped on Nyack and Coal Creek before the area was made a park, and was one of the first park rangers after the park was established in 1910.

ELIZABETH LAKE — Lakes Helen and Elizabeth were named by one of the surveyors with the U. S. Geological Survey when the area was first mapped, after his two daughters. This is shown as "Lake Jean" on a map made by Lt. George P. Ahern in 1891.

ELLEN WILSON, LAKE — Named by Secretary of the Interior Franklin K. Lane for the wife of former President Woodrow Wilson. This lake was often called "Lake Louise" by the old timers in the area.

ELLSWORTH, MT. — Named for "Billy" Ellsworth, an oldtimer who packed for the U. S. Geological Survey and who also worked on the Sperry Trail with Dr. Sperry's crew around the turn of the century.

EVANGELINE LAKE — Named by members of R. H. Sargent's survey party, 1900 to 1904, in honor of the poet Longfellow, author of the poem "Evangeline." The lake is on the slopes of Longfellow Peak.

FISHERCAP LAKE — Fishercap was the name given to George Bird Grinnell by the Blackfeet Indians.

FRANCES LAKE — Named for the wife of a member of the Northern Boundary Survey.

FUSILLADE MOUNTAIN — Named by George Bird Grinnell in 1891 as a satirical gesture at W. H. Seward and Henry L. Stimson for firing a futile volley at a group of goats on the side of this mountain.

GARDEN WALL — This long, knife-edged ridge, forming that section of the Continental Divide between Logan and Swiftcurrent Passes, was so named by one of George Bird Grinnell's parties which was camped at Grinnell Lake in the late 1890's. One evening, around a campfire, they were singing the currently popular song, "Over the Garden Wall," when one of the party remarked, "There is one wall we cannot get over," and the name was immediately applied to the ridge.

GEDUHN, MT. — Named for an early pioneer, Frank Geduhn, who had cabins for visitors at the head of Lake McDonald prior to 1900, and who guided the Sperry parties on some of their trips into the area.

GLENNS LAKE—Named for T. C. Glenns, who was born on an Indian reservation and who became station assistant and recorder to Mr. Sargent, U. S. Geological Survey topographer. G. B. Grinnell's map of 1892 shows this lake, along with Crossley Lake as "Lansing Lakes."

GOING-TO-THE-SUN MOUNTAIN — The mountain was named by James Willard Schultz for what he claimed was an old Indian legend, in which Napi, the Old Man, came down from his home in the sun to help his people, the Blackfeet, out of their difficulties. When his work was done, he returned to his home in the sun, up the slopes of this mountain. This legend however, was probably invented by the white men, and may have originated with Schultz, who was not above flowering up his stories to make them have more reader appeal.

GOULD, MT. — For G. H. Gould of Santa Barbara, California, a hunting companion of G. B. Grinnell.

GRINNELL GLACIER (Falls, Lake, Mt., Point)—In 1887 George Bird Grinnell, the man who was primarily responsible for the creation of Glacier National Park, made his second trip into the area on a hunting and exploration journey. On this trip he traveled up the Swiftcurrent Valley to what is now Swiftcurrent Lake, where he camped. There he noted the immense glaciers at the heads of the valleys and set out to explore them. On the trip to Grinnell Glacier he was accompanied by Lt. J. H. Beacom and James Willard Schultz, the first white men to set foot upon this immense body of ice, and while there Beacom named the glacier for him. The other features were later named to correspond. Grinnell Point was at one time known as Stark Peak, for Parley Stark, an early day miner who had a claim on the side of the mountain.

GUNSIGHT PASS (Mountain, Lake) — Named in 1891 by G. B. Grinnell for its resemblance to the rear sight of a rifle, with the peak of a distant mountain showing through it like the front sight. On F. E. Matthes' first maps for the Geological Survey, this peak was called Mt. Comeau, probably for Denny Comeau, an early settler at the head of Lake McDonald.

HEAVENS PEAK — A descriptive name that first appears on a map prepared by Lt. George P. Ahern of the 25th Infantry, from reconnaissance maps prepared by him in 1888-1890.

HEAVY RUNNER PEAK—Named for the Blackfeet Indian Chief

112

who was massacred along with most of his encampment by Col. Eugene M. Baker's detachment on the Marias River on January 23, 1870.

HELEN LAKE (Mountain) — There are two sources given for this name. James Willard Schultz states that it was named for Miss Helen Clark, a Montana schoolteacher and eldest daughter of Malcolm Clark who was killed at his ranch near Helena by Blackfeet Indians in 1868. The other source, the Glacier Park Transport Company Manual, states that Helen and Elizabeth were daughters of a Geological Survey engineer that worked in the area when the park was first mapped. (See Elizabeth Lake)

HENKEL, MT. — Named for an early day settler on Lower St. Mary Lake, locally called "Joe Butch."

HOWE LAKE (Creek, Ridge) — Named for Charley Howe, the first homesteader at the foot of Lake McDonald, in 1892.

IPASHA PEAK (Falls, Glacier, Lake) — Named for Ipasha, Good Spotted Tail, the Mandan Indian mother of Joseph Kipp, an oldtimer in the park.

ISABEL LAKE — Named for the wife of Thomas Dawson, part-Indian guide in the early days of the park.

JACKSON, MT. (Glacier) — Named for William Jackson, famous scout and grandson of Hugh Monroe. Jackson was quarter-breed Piegan and was a scout with Captain Reno at the time of the Custer Battle, on the Little Big Horn. Named by G. B. Grinnell.

JANET LAKE — Named for the wife of a member of the Northern Boundary Survey party.

JEFFERSON PASS — Thomas "Uncle Jeff" Jefferson, for whom this pass was named, was an interesting old character who drifted into the Lake McDonald region in the early days and did packing and other odd jobs. He was a big man, about 6'6" tall, with a long white beard which he used to hide his big meerschaum pipe, letting the smoke curl up through it in a very startling manner.

JOHN F. STEVENS CANYON — Named for the Great Northern Railway Company civil engineer who located the Marias Pass for the construction of the railroad in December 1889.

JOSEPHINE LAKE — The original source of the name "Josephine" is not known, but the lake evidently received its name from the Josephine Mine, on the slopes of Grinnell Point immediately above the lake. In the early days of the park it was often referred to as "Lake Louise," and James Willard Schultz states that the Blackfeet Indians called it "Jealous Woman's Lake."

KAINA CREEK (Lake, Mountain) — Named for the Kaina, or Blood Indians, of the Blackfeet Nation. The work "Kaina" is Blackfeet for "Many Chiefs."

KAKITOS MOUNTAIN — Kakitos is the Blackfeet name for star. The mountain often resembles a three-pointed star.

KENNEDY CREEK — Named for John Kennedy, an Indian trader who built a trading post near the mouth of this creek in 1874. Shown on Lt. Robertson's map of 1887 and also on one of G. B. Grinnell's maps as "Joe's Creek," probably for Joe Kipp.

KINTLA LAKE (Creek, Glacier, Peak) — The only explanation for this name is found in a reported legend of the Kootenai Indians, to whom the word "Kintla" means "sack." It is reported by the older Indians that in the olden days in their hunting, camping and visiting trips they would cross the mountains near this point, but would never go near the water because it had been reported that one of the Indians had gone to this lake and had fallen in and disappeared, meaning that he was drowned and his body did not come back to the surface. They stated that the lake was like a sack — after you got in you could not get out.

KIPP CREEK (Mt.) — Presumed to have been named for Joe Kipp, a half-breed Indian trapper and hunter of the early days. Joe's father was Captain James Kipp, who built the trading post at Fort Piegan, at the mouth of the Marias River in 1831.

KISHENEHN CREEK — Kishenehn is the Kootenai word for "no good," but history does not record their reason for so naming this stream.

KOOTENAI PASS (Peak) — Believed to have been named for Kootenai Brown, the first ranger in charge of Waterton Lakes National Park, who is reported to have first entered the Waterton Valley over Kootenai Pass.

LEE CREEK (Ridge) — Believed to have been named for Lee Kaiser, an early day "bull whacker" who accidently shot himself near the stream. (See "Chief Mountain")

LENA LAKE — It appears that the early day topographers, when first mapping this country, had a habit of naming hitherto unnamed features for their wives, sweethearts, or daughters. Topographer Evans, of the Geological Survey, is reported to have named this lake for his wife.

LEWIS RANGE — Named for Captain Meriwether Lewis of the Lewis and Clark Expedition, who traveled up the Marias River almost to the park in 1806.

LINCOLN PEAK (Pass, Lake, Falls)—Eddie Cruger, who packed "dude" parties out from the Lake McDonald area around the turn of the

114

century, relates how he named Lincoln Peak for Mrs. Anna T. Lincoln, matron of a girls' college in Northfield, Minnesota, who came out during the summer of 1899. Eddie guided the party to the Sperry area, where they hiked and climbed most of the peaks in the vicinity. Mrs. Lincoln could not hike or climb with the remainder of the party, so Eddie took her to Lincoln Pass, from where they made the easy ascent of Lincoln Peak. There Eddie named the peak for her. The other adjacent features evidently derived their names from the peak. Lincoln Lake was at one time called "Little St. Mary Lake," and Lincoln Falls was changed to "Beaver Chief Falls" in 1939 or 1940.

LITTLE CHIEF MOUNTAIN — Named by G. B. Grinnell in 1887 in honor of Major Frank North (Little Chief), Chief of the Pawnee Scouts in Nebraska during the 1860's.

LITTLE DOG MOUNTAIN — Named by G. B. Grinnell for "Little Dog," the Blackfeet Indian Chief who, in 1853, told Isaac Stevens, the new Governor of the Washington Territory, of the existence of Marias Pass, and started the search for it that lasted until its exploration by John F. Stevens in 1889.

LOGAN PASS (Creek, Mountain) — Named for Major Wm. R. Logan, first superintendent of Glacier National Park, from 1910 to 1912.

LOGGING CREEK (Lake, Mountain, Ridge) — So named because of extensive logging operations along the lower reaches of the creek prior to the time the area was made into a park. Early records indicate that a man by the name of Chisholm cut out a large number of yellow pine logs in the area in 1891 or 1892, and decked them in a dry wash near the river, expecting high water to take them out and down the river. Evidently the river never came this high, for the remains of these log decks may still be seen, not far from the Logging Ranger Station.

LONEMAN MOUNTAIN — Named by James Willard Schultz for a noted member of the Blackfeet Indian tribe. The name was given to the mountain on a trip up the Nyack Valley in 1902, accompanied by Joseph Kipp, Wm. Jackson and the noted writer, Emerson Hough.

LONE WALKER MOUNTAIN — Named for Lone Walker, a great Blackfeet chief and father-in-law of Hugh Monroe, to whose band Monroe first attached himself when coming into the Blackfeet country.

LONGFELLOW PEAK (Creek) — Named by R. H. Sargent, topographer for the Geological Survey in the early day mapping of the park, in honor of poet Henry Wadsworth Longfellow. Evangeline Lake is on the slopes of this peak.

McCLINTOCK PEAK — Named for Walter McClintock, author of "The Old North Trail," a story of early life with the Blackfeet.

McDONALD, LAKE (Creek, Falls) — In about the year 1878, Duncan McDonald, son of a Hudson's Bay Company factor, Angus McDonald, visited this lake, which was then known as "Terry Lake," for General Terry, an outstanding Indian fighter of the west. Duncan, who had the job of freighting a large amount of supplies to Canada, had intended to go up the North Fork of the Flathead, probably over the present Kishenehn trail route, but, upon finding his way blocked by a band of unfriendly Indians, he swung eastward and started up the next adjacent valley paralleling the North Fork. At the close of day, accompanied by a group of Flathead Indians, he came to the shores of this lake and camped there overnight. While in camp that evening he carved his name upon the bark of a birch tree. The next day he continued his journey, reaching Canada safely. The tree bearing his name remained for many years near the present village of Apgar. People who saw the name on the tree gradually began to call it McDonald's Lake," and so the name became fixed.

McPARTLAND MOUNTAIN — Believed to have been named for Frank McPartland, of eastern Montana, who worked around Lake McDonald for two seasons and was drowned in a boating accident on the lake in the 1890's.

MARIAS (Muh-RYE-us) — This pass derived its name from the Marias River, one branch of which heads in the pass. The river, in turn, was so-named in 1805 by Captain Meriwether Lewis of the Lewis and Clark Expedition, in honor of Miss Maria Wood, cousin of Captain Clark. The Flathead Indians called it "Eneas Pass," for Chief Eneas, but the Blackfeet called it the "Big Gap."

MATAHPI PEAK — The name, meaning "Face Mountain," was the old Blackfeet name for Going-to-the-Sun Mountain, because of the snow field that resembles the head of an Indian Chief near the eastern summit of the latter peak, when viewed from the east at certain times of the year. The name was erroneously applied by white men to the small peak immediately north of Going-to-the-Sun Mountain.

MEDICINE GRIZZLY LAKE — Named for the legendary "Medicine Grizzly" which inhabited Cut Bank Valley, and whose story is told in McClintock's "Old North Trail." This grizzly was reported killed by Chance Beebe, U. S. Biological Survey hunter from Columbia Falls, Montana.

MERRITT, MT. — Named for General Wesley Merritt, U. S. Army.

MICHE WABUN LAKE (Falls, Glacier, Peak) — Named from the Cree Indian name of the Great White Rabbit, once the great sun god of the Crees.

MORNING STAR LAKE — Named for an Indian princess whose story is told in McClintock's "Old North Trail."

NORRIS MOUNTAIN — Named by G. B. Grinnell for Hank Norris, a squaw man who became a member of the Blackfeet tribe, and was a noted mountaineer and hunter. Norris was reported to have owned all the allotment between the two St. Mary Lakes before the park was created, and was one of the men responsible for the naming of Cracker Lake.

NYACK CREEK — Origin of this name is unknown, although used for this stream prior to 1910. It has also been called "Mud Creek" (Major Logan) and "Gibbon Creek" (F. E. Matthes).

OBERLIN, MT. (Falls) — Named by Dr. L. B. Sperry for Oberlin College. Oberlin Falls was later re-named "Birdwoman Falls."

OLD SUN GLACIER — Named for Old Sun, or Ntas, great sun priest of the Blackfeet. This name was suggested by J. W. Schultz for Mt. Merritt, upon whose flank this glacier rests.

OTATSO CREEK (Lake) — "Otatso" is the Blackfeet word for "Walking Stooped," the Indian name for John Kennedy, who built a trading post at the mouth of Kennedy Creek. For many years this creek was known as "Kennedy Creek" or the "North Fork of Kennedy Creek."

OTOKOMI MOUNTAIN (Lake) — Named by G. B. Grinnell for Otokomi (Yellowfish), a part Blackfeet Indian who accompanied Grinnell on his early expeditions into this region. Otokomi's English name was Rose, so Roes Basin and Roes Creek nearby resulted from a misspelling of his name. Early topographers sometimes called this mountain "Whitefish" Mountain, probably an erroneous translation of "Otokomi."

PARKE PEAK (Creek, Ridge) — Named for John G. Parke, chief astronomer for the International Boundary Survey party.

PIEGAN MOUNTAIN (Falls, Glacier, Pass) — Named by James Willard Schultz in 1885 for the Piegan tribe of the Blackfeet Indian Nation.

PINCHOT, MT. (Creek) — Named for Gifford Pinchot, forester and first chief of the United States Forest Service.

PITAMAKAN PASS (Lake) — Named for Running Eagle (Pitamakan), the Blackfeet Joan of Arc. Running Eagle was a warrior girl that led war parties on many highly successful raids and was the only woman in the Blackfeet tribe ever to do so or to be given a man's name. Pitamakan Pass was originally named Cut Bank Pass, but the latter name was given to the pass between Mt. Morgan and Flinsch Peak.

POLLOCK MOUNTAIN—Named by Ross Carter for W. C. Pollack, a member of the Indian Commission appointed by the Secretary of the Interior to buy from the Indians the strip of land along the eastern side of the Rockies.

117

PUMPELLY GLACIER (Pillar) — Named for Raphael Pumpelly of Newport, R. I., leader of the Northern Transcontinental Railway Survey party that crossed Pitamakan Pass in 1883. On this trip was Major Logan, who later became the first superintendent of Glacier National Park.

RED EAGLE MOUNTAIN (Creek, Glacier, Lake, Pass) — James Willard Schultz states that the name was given to the mountain by his Indian wife in 1887, for her uncle, Red Eagle, who had saved their son's life with his prayers to the Sun.

REUTER PEAK — Probably named for Jack Reuter, an old-timer who settled on Big Prairie, on the North Fork not far from the foot of this peak.

REYNOLDS MOUNTAIN (Creek) Named by George Bird Grinnell for a member of his "Forest and Stream" staff.

RISING WOLF MOUNTAIN—Rising Wolf was the Indian name for Hugh Monroe, the first white man to live with the Blackfeet Indians. The name is said to have been suggested by Monroe's habit of getting out of bed in the morning on his hands and knees.

ROES BASIN (Creek) — Named for Otokomi (Yellowfish), a part Blackfeet Indian who accompanied G. B. Grinnell on his early expeditions into this region. Otokomi's English name was Rose, but early cartographers misspelled it as Roes, and Roes Creek and Roes Basin were the result. Roes Lake was later renamed Otokomi.

RUGER LAKE — Named for Thomas H. Ruger, a Civil War general who commanded a large part of the Dakota and Montana territory around 1890.

ST. MARY LAKE (Falls, River) — There is much controversy over the origin of this name as applied to St. Mary Lakes. J. W. Schultz states that Father Pierre DeSmet, the Belgian Missionary named the lakes, but DeSmet's papers and records do not indicate that he ever reached the lake. Other accounts state that the name was given to the St. Mary River by the International Boundary Survey party in 1870. It is more probable that the name was given by Hugh Monroe, the first white man to live with the Blackfeet Indians, probably shortly after first arriving in the country in 1814.

The Piegan Indians called these lakes the "Walled-in Lakes," while the Kootenais called them "Old Woman Lakes." Mr. James Doty, one of Governor Stevens exploration party chiefs who explored and mapped much of the eastern front of the range, camped on the Lower St. Mary Lake in May 1854. He called the upper lake "Bow Lake" and the lower one "Chief Mountain Lake." Later maps of the International Boundary Commission erroneously applied the latter name to the present Waterton Lake, despite the fact that Doty specifically stated in his reports that his survey showed the lake and its environs to be wholly within American territory and more than ten miles south of the boundary. He gives the exact location. The outlet of St. Mary Lakes, now called the St. Mary River, was called Mo-Ko-Un, or "Belly River," by the Blackfeet, a name now applied to the stream farther north.

SCALPLOCK MOUNTAIN — Named for a small tuft of trees resembling an Indian's scalplock, that remained on its summit following the fire that destroyed the remaining timber.

SEWARD MOUNTAIN — Named by George Bird Grinnell for William H. Seward, Secretary of State under President Lincoln. The name was originally applied to the entire ridge from Seward Mountain, which is north and east, to Chief Mountain, previously known as "Seward's Ridge."

SHEPARD GLACIER — Named for E. R. Shepard, a photographer for the Chaney-Sperry party.

SHERBURNE LAKE (Peak) — Named for J. J. Sherburne, a secretary-treasurer of the Swiftcurrent Oil, Land and Power Co., which drilled for oil near the site of the present Sherburne Dam in 1904.

SHIELDS CREEK (Mountain) — Named for an old timer, Mr. Shields, a polished idler from Virginia whose wife ran a store at Essex, Montana.

SINGLESHOT MOUNTAIN—So named by James Willard Schultz because G. B. Grinnell is reported to have killed a running bighorn sheep there with a single shot.

SINOPAH MOUNTAIN—Sinopah, meaning "kit fox" in Blackfeet, was the Indian wife of Hugh Monroe (Rising Wolf) and daughter of Lone Walker, a powerful Blackfeet chief.

SIYEH, MT. (Creek, Glacier, Pass) — Named by G. B. Grinnell for a Blackfeet Indian, "Sai-yeh," in Blackfeet means Crazy Dog, or Mad Wolf.

SNYDER CREEK (Ridge, Lake)—George Snyder was an early settler near the head of Lake McDonald, who built the first hotel there in 1895, at the site of the present Lake McDonald Lodge. He also put the first power boat on the lake, a steamboat which he used to carry passengers to his hotel.

SPERRY GLACIER — Named for Dr. Lyman B. Sperry of Oberlin College, Ohio, the "Gentleman Explorer," who led the first party to reach the glacier in 1896, and who later was responsible for the building of the first trail to this glacier over approximately the same route as the present one.

SQUAW MOUNTAIN — A descriptive name given because of a

119

high block of stone that stands on the eastern slope of the mountain, the "Old Squaw," resembling an Indian woman wearing a shawl or blanket. Tom Dawson states that the old Indian legend tells how the squaws went up on high points to serve as lookouts and signal when the men were on a buffalo hunt, and the rock of Squaw Mountain is symbolic of the Blackfeet woman waiting with infinite patience for the return of the buffalo.

STANTON MOUNTAIN — Named for Lottie Stanton, a pioneer woman who followed the construction camps during the railroad building days.

STIMSON, MT. (Creek) — Named by G. B. Grinnell for Henry L. Stimson, later Secretary of State, who was a member of one of Grinnell's parties in 1891. The name was originally applied to the present Mt. Logan, the present Mt. Stimson then being called Mt. James. The change to the present names was probably made by the topographers when the park was mapped.

STONEY INDIAN LAKE (Pass, Peaks)—Named for the Stoney Indians, a branch of the Assiniboine Sioux.

SWIFTCURRENT CREEK (Falls, Glacier, Lake, Mountain, Pass, Ridge) — This name was originally applied to the stream by G. B. Grinnell in 1885 or 1886 after the Indian name, "Swift Flowing River." Swiftcurrent Lake was also named by Grinnell but was later changed to Lake McDermott after a local lumberman in the late 1890's, then officially changed back to Swiftcurrent in 1928. Swiftcurrent Pass was once known as Horsethief Pass, for the Blackfeet horses that were reported to have been driven over it after horse-stealing raids.

THUNDERBIRD FALLS (Glacier, Mountain) — Named for the Thunder Bird, common in the Indian myths of this region.

TINKHAM MOUNTAIN — Lieutenant A. W. Tinkham was an Army engineer sent by Governor Isaac Stevens to look for Marias Pass and who, in the fall of 1853, crossed Pitamakan Pass, thinking it was the Marias. His was the first recorded journal of the crossing of a pass in the park by a white man.

TRIPLE DIVIDE PEAK (Pass) — The waters from this peak flow into three major drainages: the Hudson's Bay, through the St. Mary and Saskatchewan; the Pacific, through the Flathead and Columbia; and the Gulf of Mexico, through the Missouri-Mississippi.

TWO MEDICINE CREEK (Lakes, Pass)—This name is reported to have been derived from the name "Two Medicine Lodge Creek," so called because at one time there were two "medicine lodges" located on either side of the creek.

VAUGHT, MT. — Named for L. O. Vaught, of Jacksonville, Illinois, who spent his summers in the park for many years.

WALTON CREEK (Mountain) — Named for the patron saint of fishermen, Izaak Walton, because of the good fishing in the area.

WATERTON LAKES (River, Valley) — These lakes were first visited by a party from the British Palliser Expedition in 1858, led by Captain T. W. Blakiston. While encamped upon the shores of the lakes, Blakiston named them for Charles Waterton, an eminent English naturalist.

WHITE CALF MOUNTAIN — Named for the last head of the Piegan Blackfeet, by the surveyors of the strip of land ceded to the U. S. Government by the Blackfeet in 1896.

WHITE QUIVER FALLS — Name suggested by H. A. Noble of the Glacier Hotel Company, after "White Quiver," the hero in a novel written by H. F. Sanders. Formerly known as "Washboard Falls."

WILBUR, MT. (Creek) — Named by G. B. Grinnell in 1885, for E. R. Wilbur, one of Grinnell's partners in the Forest and Stream Publishing Company.

WINDMAKER LAKE — Wind Maker was a mythical being of Blackfeet mythology, whose home was in the waters of this lake at the head of the Swiftcurrent Valley, and who caused the wind to blow so furiously from the mountains.

WYNN, MT. — Named for Frank B. Wynn, physician and scientist who was killed in an attempt to climb Mt. Siyeh on July 27, 1927. This mountain was originally named "Point Mountain" by George Bird Grinnell on his map of 1885-92. Later the miners from the mining town of Altyn, near the head of Sherburne Lake, named it Altyn, after their town, and in 1927 topographers transferred this name to a mountain overlooking Swiftcurrent where it remained, and renamed the former mountain, "Mt. Wynn."

FOOTNOTES

1. Lang, George W. & Revis, Kathleen, *Many-Splendored Glacierland*, National Geographic Magazine, May, 1956, p. 598.
2. Beals, Ralph L., *Earliest Glacier—A By-Passed Beaver Bonanza*, Montana, the magazine of western history, Summer, 1957, p. 4.
3. Robinson, Donald H., *Historical Notes on Glacier National Park*, p. 22.
4. Abbott, Newton Carl, *Montana in the Making*.
5. Ibid.
6. Ibid.
7. Ibid.
8. Bancroft, Hubert Howe, *The Works of Hubert Howe Bancroft*, Vol. XXXI, p. 393.

9. *Great Falls Tribune*, 1889.
10. Robinson, Donald H., *Short History of Glacier National Park*, unpublished.
11. McClintock, Walter, *Old North Trail*.
12. Steward, Julian H., *The Blackfoot*.
13. Robinson, Donald H., *Short History of Glacier National Park*, unpublished.
14. Murray, Genevieve, *Marias Pass*, p. 9.
15. Ibid, p. 13.
16. Robinson, Donald H., *Short History of Glacier National Park*, unpublished.
17. Harper, Frank B., *Fort Union and Its Neighbors*, p. 12
18. Official Records, War Department.
19. Schultz, James Willard, *Signposts of Adventure*, p. 150.
20. Grant, Madison, *History of Glacier National Park*, p. 10.
21. Sperry, Lyman B., *In the Montana Rockies*.
22. Murray, Genevieve, *Marias Pass*, p. 37.
23. Pumpelly, Raphael, *My Reminiscences*, Vol. II, p. 630-637.
24. *Weekly Missoulian*, October 5, 1883.
25. Robinson, Donald H., *Short History of Glacier National Park*, unpublished.
26. Ridenour, J. H., *The Voyage of the Steamer Oakes*.
27. Liebig, Frank F., *Early Days in the Forest Service*, U. S. F. S. — R. 1.
28. Ibid.
29. Stagner, Howard R., *The National Park Wilderness*.

SELECTED REFERENCES

ABBOTT, Newton Carl — Montana in the Making. 1939.

AHERN, Major George P., — Montana's Last Extensive Exploration. Manuscript.

ALBRIGHT, George Leslie, M. A. — Official Explorations for Pacific Railroads, 1853-1955. Univ. Calif. Press, Berkeley. 1921

APGAR SCHOOL — Apgar History. A paper on History of Apgar residents, compiled by the school at Apgar, Montana. 1950.

BANCROFT, Hubert Howe, — The Works of Hubert Howe Bancroft, Vol. XXXI. History of Washington, Idaho, and Montana, 1845-1889. The History Publishing Co., 1890.

BARRY, J. Neilson—James Doty. Letter April 19, 1935. Official GNP Files.

BARRY, J. Neilson—James Doty. Letter July 12, 1935. Official GNP Files.

BARRY, J. Neilson—Marias Pass. Letter March 11, 1929. Official GNP Files.

BEALS, Ralph L. — Earliest Glacier — A By-Passed Beaver Bonanza. Montana, the Magazine of Western History, Summer, 1957.

BEALS, Ralph L. — History of Glacier National Park with Particular Emphasis on the Northern Developments, U.S. Dept. of Int., National Park Service. Berkeley, California. 1935.

BRIMLOW, George F. — Marias Pass Explorer, John F. Stevens. Montana

Magazine of History, Historical Society of Montana, Vol. 3, No. 3, Summer, 1953, p.39.

CAMPBELL, Archibald — Reports Upon the Survey of the Boundary Between the Territory of the United States and the Possessions of Great Britain. Government Printing Office, Washington D. C., 1878.

CAMPBELL, Marius R. — The Glacier National Park, A Popular Guide to its Geology and Scenery. Govt. Printing Office, Washington, D. C., 1914.

CANADIAN CATTLEMAN — June, 1940.

COLLINS, Mrs. Nat. — The Cattle Queen. Undated publication, probably late 1880's.

CONTRIBUTIONS to the Historical Society of Montana, 1890 to 1923, Vols. 4, 5, 6, 7, 9, and 10.

CRUGER, E. J. — Personal Interview by D. H. Robinson, 1952 and 1953.

CULVER, G. E. — Notes on a Little Known Region in Northwestern Montana, Wisconsin Academy of Sciences, Arts and Letters. 1891.

DE SMET, Father Pierre — Letters and Accounts in Thwaite's, Early Western Travels. 1748-1846.

DOTY, James — Itinerary of James Doty, 1854. Pacific Railroad Reports, Vol. 1, p. 547-551. Vol. 12, p. 184-186. From letter by J. Neilson Barry, dated April 19, 1935. Official GNP Files.

DOUMA, Don—Second Bonanza: The History of Oil in Montana. Montana Magazine of History, Historical Society of Montana. Vol. 3, No. 4, Autumn, 1953.

ELROD, Morton J. — Elrod's Guide and Book of Information of Glacier National Park. M. J. Elrod. 1924.

EWERS, John C. — The Story of the Blackfeet. Indian Lore and Customs, Pamphlet No. 6. U.S. Dept. Interior, Indian Service. 1944.

FLANDRAU, Grace — The Story of Marias Pass. Great Northern Railway.

GARRISON, Lon — The Park Saddle Horse Company. Official Files GNP.

GLACIER DRIFT Nature Notes—1927 to 1936. Glacier National Park Library.

GLACIER NATIONAL PARK — Official files, 1910 to 1953. Miscellaneous letters, records, reports, etc.

GLACIER NATIONAL PARK — Official files on Cassidy-Swiftcurrent Oil Co., dated July 5, 1923; Feb. 28, 1925; May 11, 1926.

GLACIER NATIONAL PARK — Park Naturalist's Reports, 1925-1953. Official files GNP.

GLACIER NATIONAL PARK — Press Releases, various dates.

GLACIER NATIONAL PARK — Superintendent's annual & monthly reports, 1911 - 1953.

GLACIER PARK Transport Co. — Drivers' Manual. Various issues, 1937-49.

GRANT, Madison — Early History of Glacier National Park. U.S. Gov't. Printing Office. 1919.

GREAT NORTHERN Semaphore — January, 1927

GREENHOW, Robert — Memoir Historical and Political of the Northwest Coast of America. Washington, D. C. 1840.

GRINNELL, George Bird — Historic Papers of Dr. George Bird Grinnell. Bound original letters and clippings. GNP Library.

GRINNELL, George Bird — The Crown of the Continent. From the Century, Vol. 62, Sept. 1901, p. 660.

HARPER, Frank B. — Fort Union and its Neighbors., p. 12.

HOSMER, James K. — History of the Expedition of Captain Lewis and Clark, 1804-05-06. Vols. I and II. A. C. McClurg & Co. 1924

HUTCHINGS, Henry W. — Personal Interviews by D. H. Robinson, 1951.

LAUT, Agnes C. — The Blazed Trail of the Old Frontier. Robt. McBride & Co. 1926.

LANG, George W. & Revis, Kathleen — Many-Splendored Glacierland, National Geographic Magazine, May, 1956.

LIBBY, Donald C. — Letter to Kalispell News, March 18, 1929. Official GNP Files.

LIEBIG, Frank F. — Various items, diaries, albums, clippings, etc., from the collection of the late Frank F. Liebig, Kalispell, Montana.

LIEBIG, Mrs. Fiank F. — Personal Interview by D. H. Robinson, 1953.

LOGAN, Major W. R. — A National Park in its Formative Stages. From proceedings of the National Park Conference, 1911, p. 161.

MALOUF, Carling — Early Kootenai History. Montana Magazine of History, Historical Society of Montana, Vol. II, No. 2, April, 1952, p. 5.

McCLINTOCK, Walter—The Old North Trail. MacMillan & Co., London, 1910.

MIDDLETON, S. H. — Waterton-Glacier International Peace Park, GNP Library.

MONTANA Historical Society — Montana Magazine of History, Helena, Montana. 1951-1953.

MONTANA School of Mines—Librarian, Loretta B. Peck. Letter Sept. 11, 1947.

MURRAY, Genevieve — Marias Pass, Its Part in the History and Development of the Northwest. Studies in Northwest History No. 12, University of Montana, Missoula. Reprint from Great Falls Tribune, Great Falls, Montana.

NEIL, Henry — Letter to Supt. Galen, Feb. 12, 1914. Official files, GNP.

NIELSON, Charles — Personal Interview by D. H. Robinson. 1952.

NOFFSINGER, Mrs. Edwina — Personal Interview by D. H. Robinson. 1953.

OPINION — Chinook, Montana. October 29, 1892.

PLASSMAN, M. E. — Plenna Herald, September, 1924.

PUBLIC ARCHIVES of Canada —Series C., Vol. 202, p. 11. Montana Historical Library ref., Helena, Montana.

PUMPELLY, Raphael—My Reminiscenses. Henry Holt & Co., New York. 1918.

RECORD — Fort Benton, Montana. 1877.

RIDENOUR, J. H. — The Voyage of the Steamer Ookes. 1942. Official files.

RIVER PRESS — Fort Benton, Montana. February 19, 1890.

ROBINSON, Donald H. — Historical Notes on Glacier National Park.

ROBINSON, Donald H.—Short History of Glacier National Park, unpublished.

ROGERS, Edmund B. — Abstracts of Legislation in Congress Relating to the Establishment of Glacier National Park. pril, 1948. Official files, GNP.

ROGERS, Edmund B. — History of Legislation Pertaining to Glacier National Park. Letter to Supt., Glacier National Park, October 30, 1935. Official files GNP.

RUHLE, Dr. George C. — Historical Briefs, compiled by Dr. Ruhle for Glacier Park Drivers' Manual. 1949.

RUHLE, Dr. George C. — Logan Pass Dedication Ceremony, July 15, 1933. Official files GNP.

RUHLE, Dr. George C.—Various articles in Drivers' Manual and official files.

SANDERS, Helen Fitzgerald—A History of Montana. Vols. I and III. Lewis Publishing Co. 1913.

SCHULTZ, James Willard—My Life as an Indian. Houghton Mifflin Co. 1906.

SCHULTZ, James Willard — Rising Wolf, The White Blackfoot, Houghton Mifflin Co. 1919.

SCHULTZ, James Willard — Various articles written for Forest & Stream and other publications.

SCHULTZ, James Willard — Signposts of Adventure. Houghton Mifflin Co. 1926.

SCOYEN, E. T. — Letter to Mr. Clare Murphy, March 28, 1936. Official fies, GNP.

SHANNON, Frank M. — History of Glacier National Park. Great Falls Tribune, March 17, 1940, and other articles.

SHERBURNE, Frank P. —Personal Interview by D. H. Robinson, 1953.

SHERBURNE, Frank P. — Mineral and Oil Venture in Glacier National Park. History files, GNP.

SHERBURNE, J. L. — Swiftcurrent Oil Wells. Official files, GNP.

SPERRY, Albert L. — Avalanche. Christopher Publishing House. 1938.

SPERRY, Lyman B. — In the Montana Rockies.

STAGNER, Howard R. — The National Park Wilderness.

STEVENSON, Frank M. — Diary, owned by Mrs. Earl Burris, Hayden Lake, Idaho.

STEWARD, Julian H. — The Blackfoot. U. S. Dept. Int., National Park Service, Berkeley, California. 1934.

TINKHAM, Lt. A. W. — Excerpts from "Explorations and Surveys for a Railroad Route from the Mississippi River to the Pacific Ocean." Vol 1, War Department. Reprinted in Glacier Drift.

TRIBUNE — Great Falls, Montana. Various articles.

U. S. FOREST SERVICE — Early Days in the Forest Service. Region 1, U. S. F. S., Missoula, Montana, 1944. From Liebig Collection.

VAUGHT, L. O. — Letter to Dr. G. C. Ruhle, March 8, 1936. Official files, GNP.

VAUGHT, L. O. — Manuscript in history file. GNP.
VEACH, William — An Early Trip Into Glacier Park. Official files, GNP. February 22, 1929.
WEEKLY MISSOULIAN — Missoula, Montana. 1883.
WEDEMEYER, Olga — The Story of the Tobacco Plains Country.
WHIPPS, W. C. — Letter to Supt. Scoyen, January 23, 1933. Official GNP place names file.
WHITCRAFT, Thos. E. — Early Days in the Ranger Force—Report dated May 7, 1935. Official files, GNP.

APPENDIX B

List of Superintendents since the Establishment of Glacier National Park

Name	Title	Period of Service
Major Wm. R. Logan	Supt. of Road & Trail Construction	8-8-10 to 12-1-10
Major Wm. R. Logan	Inspector in Charge	12-1-10 to 4-1-11
Major Wm. R. Logan	Superintendent	4-1-11 to 2-7-12
Henry W. Hutchings	Acting Superintendent	2-8-12 to 5-15-12
Robert H. Chapman	Acting Superintendent	5-16-12 to 11-30-12
James L. Galen	Superintendent	12-1-12 to 8-4-14
Samuel F. Ralston	Supervisor	8-5-14 to 6-17-17
George E. Goodwin	Acting Supervisor	6-18-17 to 8-15-17
Walter W. Payne	Superintendent	8-16-17 to 6-30-20
George E. Goodwin	Acting Superintendent	7-1-20 to 11-30-20
Henry W. Hutchings	Acting Superintendent	12-1-20 to 5-11-21
J. Ross Eakin	Superintendent	5-12-21 to 1-9-24
Henry W. Hutchings	Acting Superintendent	1-10-24 to 1-24-24
Charles J. Kraebel	Superintendent	1-25-24 to 2-25-27
Raymond R. Vincent	Acting Superintendent	2-26-27 to 4-10-27
J. Ross Eakin	Superintendent	4-11-27 to 1-15-31
Eivind T. Scoyen	Superintendent	1-16-31 to 12-31-38
Donald S. Libby	Superintendent	1-1-39 to 8-25-44
John W. Emmert	Superintendent	9-1-44 to 3-31-58
Stanley C. Joseph	Acting Superintendent	4-1-58 to 6-10-58
Edward A. Hummel	Superintendent	6-1-58 to 9-17-62
Harthon L. Bill	Superintendent	10-14-62 to 3-14-64
Keith Neilson	Superintendent	3-15-64 to 7-12-69
William Briggle	Superintendent	7-13-69 to date

APPENDIX C
List of Principal Interpretive Personnel under the National Park Service

Name	Title	Period of Service
Morton J. Elrod	Nature Guide	1922 to 1926
Morton J. Elrod	Ranger Naturalist	1926 to 1928
George C. Ruhle	Park Naturalist	1929 to 1941
Merle V. Walker	Chief Park Naturalist	1941 to 1944
Matthew E. Beatty	Chief Park Naturalist	1944 to1955
Harry B. Robinson	Chief Park Naturalist	1955 to 1958
Francis H. Elmore	Chief Park Naturalist	1958 to 1970
Edwin L. Rothfuss	Chief Park Naturalist	1971 to present

APPENDIX D

Year	Visitors	Rail Arrivals	Year	Visitors	Rail Arrivals
1911	4,000		1942	63,080	3,740
1912	6,257		1943	23,496 (3)	4
1912	12,138		1944	36,192	0—War
1914	12,168		1945	67,179	0—Years
1915	13,465		1946	201,145	7,496
1916	12,839		1947	324,396 (4)	9,679
1917	15,050		1948	281,562	7,870
1918	9,086 (1)		1949	478,839	7,805
1919	18,956		1950	485,950	9,072
1920	22,449		1951	500,125	6,479
1921	19,736		1952	630,949	5,738
1922	23,935		1953	633,480	12,094
1923	33,988		1954	608,230	7,737
1924	33,372		1955	674,004	7,795
1925	40,063		1956	718,939	9,325
1926	36,901		1957	759,161	8,087
1927	41,745	8,856	1958	706,841	5,245
1928	53,454	9,401	1959	722,338	6,341
1929	70,742	10,182	1960	724,538	8,254
1930	73,783	8,432	1961	739,982	4,808
1931	59,846	6,056	1962	966,100	9,364
1932	53,202	2,988	1963	811,214 (5)	3,893
1933	76,615	3,852	1964	642,184	4,260
1964	116,965	6,743	1965	847,104 (6)	3,521
1935	143,240	7,698	1966	907,839	3,286
1936	210,072	9,100	1967	884,049 (7)	
1937	194,522	8,655	1968	964,493	
1938	153,528 (2)	8,305	1969	1,051,165	
1939	170,073	7,644	1970	1,241,603	
1940	177,307	7,950	1971	1,303,073	
1941	179,082	9,246	1972	1,392,145	

(1) World War I
(2) Change in method of recording visitors using actual count only.
(3) Beginning of World War II and travel curtailment.

(4) End of travel curtailment.
(5) Year of Seattle World's Fair.
(6) Year of major flood
(7) No rail arrival statistics available after this date.

History/Glacier National Park

For a window to the history of interpretation in the park, the Glacier Association is proud to bring you this special edition of the 1960s classic *THROUGH THE YEARS IN GLACIER NATIONAL PARK.*

THROUGH THE YEARS is presented in its last printed edition without filtering of the modern lense. Packed with an "administrative" history of the park from 1910 to 1960, *THROUGH THE YEARS* features thirty-one historical photographs, including the original Apgar Cabin, Old McCarthyville, the former town of Altyn, the original Snyder Hotel, the dedication ceremony at Logan Pass for the opening of the Going-to-the-Sun Road and many others. This historic text displays careful management and documentation of this precious resource, preserved much as it is today.

Glacier
Association

ISBN 978-0-9826463-0-4

51695

9 780982 646304

US $16.95

SUN POINT
HISTORIC REPRINTS

SUNPOINTPRESS.CO